"An outstanding philosophy for everyone, it goes beyond theory, and presents practical and realistic solutions that can be easily tailored to any real-world situation. It works!"

—David Cross, Ed.D., Pilot, United Airlines;
   Adjunct Professor, Embry-Riddle Aeronautical University

"This engaging book wonderfully illustrates skills that will help you turn the conflicts of your daily life into seeds of positive change... and it shows you how to do it!"

—Tony LoRe, CEO / Founder, Youth Mentoring Connection/
   Urban Oasis, Author of *The Prospecting Planner*
   and curriculum at the Center for Entrepreneurism

"*Have a Nice Conflict* does a superb job of distilling key personnel concepts into a succinct format that will be of great benefit to managers and employees alike. This narrative volume presents the enduring management principles of psychologist Elias Porter in an eminently sensible and approachable way. The authors use a case example to illuminate fundamental concepts in a manner that is both compelling and readable. A definite addition to the personnel management bookshelf."

—Morgan T. Sammons, Ph.D., ABPP, Dean,
   California School of Professional Psychology

"As a Leadership Professor and Corporate Trainer, I had always believed that Emotional Intelligence was something you are born with. I believe, this book now affirms that E. I. can be learned, enhanced and that it can be developed like any other skill."

—Dr. S. Jeannette Guignard, Corporate Training Instructor,
   Chaffey College and Business & Management Instructor,
   UC Riverside Extension

"With many of the latest popular business books, I fail to make the link from theory to the practical application of their contents. Because of the storybook format and application to relationships beyond business in *Have a Nice Conflict*, the link from theoretical to practical was obvious. Once I began seeing myself in the behaviors of one of the main characters, I couldn't put it down!"

—Jonathan McGrael, Director of Training and Development, Arbor Pharmaceuticals

"*Have a Nice Conflict* offers a refreshingly candid look at conflict—both internal and interpersonal—with practical tips on how to more effectively navigate the conflict in your life."

—Judy Rannow, Professional Development Consultant, former Director of Workforce Development, Portage County Business Council Foundation

"Parables are powerful learning opportunities and have been for thousands of years. *Have a Nice Conflict* is no exception! This book helps us understand conflict—the motivation, the behaviors, and the emotions that go along with it—and then capitalize on the incredible opportunity to improve our relationships and create the results we desire most. A very compelling read!"

—Stephen E. Childs, Principle, 4R Learning Solutions

"*Have a Nice Conflict* is the perfect resource to use in working with student groups, faculty and staff. The authors weave the theory and its practical application in a wonderful and humorous story. As the student disciplinary officer of the college, it is also a helpful tool in mediating conflict to a successful outcome for all parties involved."

—Dr. Nikki Schaper, Associate Dean of Student Services, MiraCosta College, CA

"Conflict surrounds us every day in our business and personal lives. *Have a Nice Conflict* enables the reader to understand the source of these conflicts and the tools that can be used to avoid and address conflict that leads to more fulfilling relationships and positive outcomes."

—Jeff Tucker, Partner, Advantage Performance Group

"This book tells a compelling story that will surely change how you view conflict. You will recognize conflict as a natural occurrence and one that—if leveraged effectively—can result in stronger relationships and give you a unique skill set to use both professionally and personally."

—Rob McCune, Senior Consultant, Delta Point Inc.

"This little book is deceptive in its brevity for it contains powerful tools for navigating conflict. *Have a Nice Conflict* brings clarity to the often enigmatic world of relationships. The concepts in this book are profoundly accessible and thought provoking. As a project manager this book has brought tremendous value to establishing and maintaining healthy working relationships. Whether you are looking to improve job effectiveness or your personal relationships, *Have a Nice Conflict* offers powerful tools for transformation. You owe it to yourself to read this book!"

—Amber Chapman, Senior Project Manager,
Takeda Pharmaceuticals

Have a Nice CONFLICT

A Story of Finding Success & Satisfaction
in the Most Unlikely Places

TIM SCUDDER,
MICHAEL PATTERSON,
and
KENT MITCHELL

PERSONAL
STRENGTHS
PUBLISHING

Personal Strengths Publishing, Inc.
P.O. Box 2605
Carlsbad, CA 92018 USA

SDI®, Strength Deployment Inventory®, Relationship Awareness®, Have a Nice Conflict™, and the SDI Triangle are trademarks and part of the trade dress of Personal Strengths Publishing, Inc.

www.PersonalStrengths.com

FIRST EDITION

Designed by Kent Mitchell
Printed in the United States of America

CATALOGING-IN-PUBLICATION DATA

Scudder, Tim.
   Have a nice conflict: a story of finding success & satisfaction in the most unlikely
      places / Tim Scudder, Michael Patterson, Kent Mitchell
      p.   cm.
   Includes notes and bibliographical references.
   ISBN 978-1-932627-11-4
   1. Interpersonal Relations. 2. Leadership. 3. Management. 4. Employee
Motivation.   I. Title.

PUBLISHER'S NOTE

This is a work of fiction. Names, characters, places, and incidents either are the products of the authors' imagination or are used fictitiously, and any resemblance to actual persons, living or dead, events, or locales is entirely coincidental.

A word of thanks...

First and foremost, this book would not be
possible without the invaluable and practical
theory of Relationship Awareness® developed by
Elias H. Porter, Ph.D (1914-1987). Each of us
has devoted a significant portion of our careers
applying these concepts with people in all walks
of life and all types of organizations. We are most
grateful to the many people who invited us into
their organizations and allowed us to learn with
them on difficult interpersonal conflicts.

Tim Scudder

Mike Patterson

Kent Mitchell

Contents

INTRODUCTION

IN THE STORY that follows, we explore the practical ideas of Relationship Awareness Theory. While this tale is pure fiction, the situations are inspired by our real-world experiences in personal and organizational development—and life in general.

It is our hope that this book will make accessible to you some of the principles of managing conflict effectively. And when we say *effective*, we mean in ways that not only resolve the problem, but also enhance the relationships of the people involved. We further hope that you will discover a new understanding of people and learn new techniques that can reduce the amount of conflict you experience in your life.

Much of this story focuses on the workplace. But as you will soon see, the principles of conflict management explored here apply to the entire spectrum of your relationships—personal and professional.

Relationship Awareness Theory was developed over forty years ago and is being applied in some of the world's largest organizations. Those that are familiar with the theory (and the tools which are based on it) may enjoy referring to the material that follows the story where we have visually provided the motivational value systems and conflict sequences of our characters. And if you are not familiar with the theory, don't worry. That's about to change...

Thank you for reading this book. We trust you will find something useful on this journey—something that will help make your next conflict a *nice* conflict.

Have a Nice
CONFLICT

ONE

I T WAS EXACTLY 3:07 in the afternoon when John Doyle concluded that this was the worst day of his career. He could barely feel his feet hitting the floor as he retreated to his office which now felt like a hundred grueling miles from the Human Resources department. As he weaved his way through the bustling office building, the HR manager's words echoed ominously in his head until they lost all form and meaning. From her very first words, he knew what she was going to say. He could see it in her face as she rattled off the obligatory pleasantries. It felt like an eternity before she got around to the point, and it was all he could do to not walk out. Yet, somehow, he sat there, on the edge of his seat, praying he was wrong.

Finally, her face contorted—a tortured look he was sure she had practiced in the mirror before he came in. "I'm sorry, John. You were not selected for promotion at this time." The words that followed may as well have been in Swahili. They bounced off of him and littered the floor. Her weak offers of constructive feedback were no match for the tornado raging in John's head as thoughts of panic, embarrassment, exhaustion, and anger swirled with ferocious intensity.

Now he was walking through the crowded bullpen of the sales department, his face burning, his limbs tingling. Did they know? Were they staring? The infamous grapevine of Starr Industries was quite clear on the matter. Although not an official policy, John knew that there was a "three strike" rule in the company. Get passed over for promotion three times, and you might as well start looking for other options. You were damaged goods as far as senior management was concerned. John had just sat through his second strike. If he could bring himself to look around, he was sure he'd recognize the looks on his coworkers' faces. They were watching a man whose career was racing toward a brick wall.

"How did it go?" The mere sound of Cassie's voice made John nauseous.

Without even a glance at his sales assistant, he passed her desk and closed himself in his office. He hated that Cassie knew his schedule. Granted, it was her job to know, but now, he just wanted to be anonymous—to be anywhere but here. He wanted today to have been a bad dream. He was anxious to wake up, wipe the sweat from his brow, and turn over.

But while today had been a nightmare, he was very much awake. His visit to HR was only the most recent gut punch in a day full of them. John collapsed in his chair and stared at the wall. It wasn't lost on him that a promotion to regional sales manager would surely have meant an office with a window. For now he had a wall. For light, he had the humming fluorescent tubes above him. He wondered if they were content with the mediocrity with which they manufactured light. He hated mediocrity. And to find himself bathed in it—confined by it—only served to pour salt on his wounds.

He had always been proud of his life's trajectory and his steady rise through the ranks. Working constantly and driving hard for results had been his standard approach since college, and up until recently, it seemed to be working. No one had ever questioned John's commitment to the job or even his ability to deliver results, but now, that didn't seem to be enough. Somewhere along the way, he'd been derailed. He just couldn't seem to break through this last, unknown barrier that was preventing him from moving up. What was he doing wrong?

As the clock closed in on four, he thought of his family. How could he face them? In a few short hours, he would have no choice. It was J.J.'s first home game that night, and Nancy would have made sure that everyone would be taken care of. The home of Saint Nancy—as he jokingly called her—was a warm sanctuary where no child or husband was without proper nutrition and clean socks. He knew she would take the bad news with cheery, uplifting words of support, but it made him no more eager to admit his failure. Being late to the game? This is what made John most nervous. He was sickened by the irony that his drive for success at Starr Industries had taken an obvious toll on his family. And he knew Saint Nancy well enough to recognize that Mt. Saint Helens was only a tremor away when it came to John performing his responsibility as an active participant in the family.

Looking down at the papers on his desk, he was jolted out of his thoughts. Round one of the day's lopsided boxing bout had begun with a sucker-punch the second he entered his office for the day. A simple piece of paper was laid neatly on his keyboard—a faxed copy of Holly Styles' letter of resignation. John had felt the wind knocked out of him after reading only half a sentence.

Holly was John's top performing sales representative for three years running and an informal leader on the team. With her departure, John prayed that Holly had found a job in an unrelated industry, but he immediately began to worry that she had been lured away by a competitor. He began to calculate just how many customers might follow Holly to her new company and how hard it would be to find another salesperson with Holly's skill and ability to build relationships with clients. More than anything, John worried about how her departure would look in the eyes of senior management—especially since this was the second superstar John had lost in as many months.

John checked his desk phone. The voicemail indicator remained dark. Why hadn't Holly returned his calls? Throughout the day, he had left messages on her cell phone, but so far, radio silence. He racked his brain, trying to recall any warning signs he might have missed. He had no idea she was unhappy or had intended to leave. She was making great money and had a number of large deals in the sales pipeline. Nothing made sense. Had he been too hard on her? Pushed her too much?

The 9 a.m. teleconference with his team had been notably awkward. Several people asked why Holly was not on the call, and John felt a bit guilty playing dumb about it. He hadn't felt prepared to share the bad news. He knew there were rumors floating around about other team members shopping their resumes, and he worried that Holly's abrupt departure might fuel the flames of discontent. He would need to approach that announcement carefully. Then again, maybe they all knew. Maybe that's why everyone was so quiet on the call. Did they know their boss was lying?

Round three began around 10:30 a.m., as John finally mustered the courage to call his manager, Gail, to tell her that he had lost yet another top performer. Even though Gail was not the shouting type, John could hear the disappointment in the stilted gaps of silence. He couldn't help feeling like a school boy in the principal's office as she commenced a relentless inquisition about what had happened: How was he going to position this with the rest of the team? What was he doing about Holly's top five accounts? What signs of Holly's resignation should he have seen? None of his answers seemed good enough for Gail, so the 20 minute conversation felt like two hours.

It was round four with the HR manager that most left him reeling. His career aspirations were slipping through his fingers. Everything he had been working so hard for all these years and the toll it had taken on his family and his friendships now seemed wasted.

He found himself pacing when the bell rang in round five. It was the alert chime from his e-mail. He prayed it was spam. On a day like today, black market pharmaceuticals and shady investment advice would be a welcome change of pace. John clicked on the e-mail icon on his computer and discovered several new messages. One subject line caught his eye: *Exit Interview Results*.

Opening the message, he could see the report was for Andy Ward, the sales rep he had lost about six weeks ago. His HR representative was required to pass along feedback received during Andy's exit interview. John felt sick to his stomach as he read the results. *"I liked the company, and I liked the work, but I didn't like working for John. He didn't make me feel like I was part of a team. It always felt like a competition. I hate to say this, but John Doyle was the main reason I started looking for another job."*

John burned with feelings of betrayal. Andy had

fabricated some excuse about wanting to start his own business. The whole departure had been very upbeat and civilized. John had even offered to serve as a reference for him. Now, he knew the truth, and he wasn't the only one. Surely, this report was contributing to John's ever-diminishing career prospects. The pounding of John's heart seemed to shake his whole body.

There was a timid knock on his door that he knew to be Cassie's. John closed out of his e-mail program and tried to compose himself. "What?"

Cassie poked her head in. "May I?"

John waved an arm, motioning her in.

"Sorry to bug you. It's just—I didn't know if you wanted me to do anything," said Cassie.

"About what?" John had been assaulted from so many fronts; he couldn't imagine what she was talking about.

"About Holly," she said. "A few clients have called. I'm not quite sure what I should be telling them."

Something inside of John snapped into place. A surge of adrenaline seemed to seize him, dragging his body from the dark caverns of his mind. It was time for action. If he was going to survive this day, he'd have to step up and start swinging.

"Route her calls to me," he said. "In the meantime, I need you to print me a list of her clients with contact information and annual sales."

He grabbed the phone and began to dial.

"Year-to-date?" she asked, as she made her way to the door. But he had already turned away. With a roll of her eyes, Cassie left him alone.

"Hi. Walter Freeman, please," he said into the phone. "Yes, John Doyle."

John's knee began to bounce rapidly, as he was put on hold. Walter Freeman was John's oldest customer—and his biggest. John had landed the account as a hungry, naïve young kid, right out of college. Walter had relented to John's persistence, mostly because he was entertained by him—impressed by his "gumption." In the years that followed, Walter had become something of a mentor and friend. John was a frequent guest at business parties, and Walter had even invited him and Nancy to join him for an overnight cruise on his yacht. But that was years ago. John's rise to sales manager left little time for account management, so he placed Walter's business in the capable hands of his brightest salesman. But six weeks earlier, John had been forced to explain to Walter why Andy would no longer be representing his account. And as luck would have it, Holly had been Andy's replacement. It was time for major damage control.

The other line was answered by Walter's assistant. "Walter Freeman's office."

"Hi, Florence. It's John Doyle. Can I speak to Walter?"

"I'm afraid not. He's in a meeting."

"Do you know when he'll be out?"

"4:30, but he won't be able to call you back. He's jumping straight into a taxi to make a 6:30 to Chicago."

John placed the receiver to his forehead, squinting in frustration.

"I can leave him a message," she offered, apologetically.

John looked at his watch and hung up the phone. He haphazardly tossed the array of papers from his desk into his briefcase and launched from his chair.

* * *

John drummed the steering wheel of his aging BMW. There was no music, only the endless monologue of his thoughts, drowning out the muffled noise of the city streets surrounding his parked car. The downtown headquarters of Freeman-Davis Group occupied a building that stretched well above John's line of sight. In his parking spot near the main entrance, he began to wonder if this was what a stalker felt like—an uneasy fusion of adrenaline and boredom.

He debated how Walter might interpret his unannounced appearance. In the end, though, John figured it was this kind of assertiveness that cemented their personal and professional relationship in the first place. And the fact was John couldn't afford to lose Walter's business.

Finally, he saw the old man push through the front doors. Walter had to be 70 years-old by now, but he still exuded that special something that made people look his way and ask, "Who's that guy?" John often wondered whether this aura came as a result of Walter's success or whether it was the *reason* for his success. Either way, it was impressive to behold.

John got out of his car just as Walter's taxi pulled up to the curb.

"Mr. Freeman!" John shouted. The street noise was louder than he had realized. He began to jog. "Walter!"

The taxi driver was taking the suitcase before Walter noticed John approaching.

"My God, Johnny. Is that you?"

"How are you, sir?" John asked as Walter offered a hug.

"Fine. Just fine," he replied. "What are you doing on this side of town?"

"I was hoping to talk to you."

"No can do, son. Got a plane to catch."

"Let me drive you," John replied.

The taxi driver was about to close the lid of the trunk. He shot dagger eyes at John. "Naw, naw, naw. No way, man."

John shoved two 20s into the driver's shirt pocket and yanked Walter's suitcase from the trunk.

* * *

John eased his car onto the clogged freeway and cursed under his breath. Walter was watching him; John could feel it. He glanced over and saw the calm smirk of a man who expected everything to go his way and was rarely proved wrong.

"Sir?"

"Why are you really here?" Walter asked, studying John's face.

"I just felt really terrible about—"

Walter interrupted. "Yeah, yeah. Holly flew the coop. You feel like a schmuck. I heard you the first time." Walter had a way of being brutally honest that somehow made you feel completely safe, yet completely exposed. "What went wrong with Holly?"

"I honestly don't know," John admitted, his tone a little too defensive for his own taste. "She was making a boatload of money. Topped all the sales contests. I told her every day she was a superstar. Hell, that's why I wanted her on your account."

"Is she you?"

"Excuse me?"

"You just listed off all the reasons she should have been happy with her job," Walter explained, "but those are your reasons. What were her reasons? What were the other kid's reasons?"

"Andy?"

"Was he you?"

"No," John exclaimed, frustrated. "It's sales, Walter. It's goal, target, lock n' load..."

"To you."

"Well, that's the most effective way."

Walter smiled and watched the lane of cars next to him ease slowly by.

John hated the riddles. Why couldn't people just say what they meant? Walter made you work for everything. John imagined that he made panhandlers answer questions before dropping a dollar bill in their cup. Now, Walter's silence was killing him. "Well, isn't it?" John asked.

"All I know is you're quickly running out of soldiers, Lieutenant."

The rest of the trip was silent. Not because John was angry but because he was again deep in his own head orchestrating a rampant flurry of thoughts and internal debates. As they pulled up to the curb next to the sky-cap, Walter pulled a business card from his suit pocket, flipped it over and began to write.

"You want to know the secret to success, son?"

"A creative CPA?" John joked.

Walter finished writing and clicked his pen. "Strategy, diplomas, business plans, loopholes in the federal tax code... all great. Important stuff. But the lifeblood of any organization is people. Our lives in general are all about people. You got conflict in your life? You're choking off your blood supply. Your success is going to turn blue and fall off. By the looks of it, I'd say it's already looking a bit periwinkle."

Walter handed John the card and climbed out of the

car. On the back Walter had written a phone number followed by the words: *Have a Nice Conflict.* John groaned at the sight of another damn riddle. Walter dragged his suitcase out of the back seat.

"What's this supposed to be?" John asked through the open door.

"Tell them I sent you."

"Tell who?"

"Thanks for the ride, Johnny," he said, wearing a wry grin. "Enjoy yours."

With a tap of the roof, Walter turned and disappeared into the crowded terminal.

TWO

IT DIDN'T LOOK LIKE MUCH, but the pale, wet hot dog was all John had time for. He accepted it from the vendor with a frown. John's phone was wedged precariously between his ear and shoulder, as he slathered on the mustard and ketchup. On the other end of the call was his manager, Gail. It was his second run-in with her since he had arrived at work that day. The dust cloud of the previous day had started to seep into her office, and she wasn't happy about it.

"You're one of my key sales managers, John," she said in a hauntingly even tone, "a key part of this system. When any part of this system breaks down, it's me who has to explain it to upper management."

"Do you think I wanted to get passed over again?"

Gail was silent. He looked at his watch. He was due for his appointment in less than 15 minutes, and all he could do was watch his meal get cold in his hand. He found an open spot on a park bench and sat down.

"I know you're a skilled salesperson," she said, finally. "One of the best I've worked with. But I'm just not sure management is where you can be most effective."

"That's not true," he countered, hoping she wouldn't push him for proof.

"There are certain people skills—"

"Sales is all about people skills," he interrupted.

She went silent. John pictured her counting to 10 in her head. "John, clearly managing people requires a certain... finesse. Building relationships... where people are motivated. Where uncomfortable situations are handled appropriately."

"I'm working on it," he said.

"How?"

He didn't fully know the answer himself. He had called the number Walter had given him but had no idea what lay before him. He despised operating this way— with his eyes closed, not in control. *Have a Nice Conflict...* that's all he had to go on. He checked his watch again. Ten minutes until his appointment. "I gotta go, Gail. Can we talk about this when I get back to the office?"

"I'll be in all afternoon," she sighed.

John hung up the phone and exhaled heavily. He finally noticed the man sitting next to him on the bench, enjoying a hot dog of his own. They exchanged a cordial nod, and John took a long awaited bite of his cold lunch.

"You know," the man said. "They say the soft stuff is harder than the hard stuff."

"Excuse me?" John asked.

"The soft skills. People skills."

John dug deep into his own skill set to keep from telling the man to mind his own business. He took another bite. "People skills," John scoffed.

"Sore subject," the man concluded. "Sorry."

"No it's just—" John could feel himself getting wound up. "If you knew this woman, you'd laugh at the thought of her preaching people skills. 'Bout as cold and reserved as you can get. She could win the lottery, and you'd be lucky to notice her raise her eyebrows." John's hot dog somersaulted to the concrete. He was known to talk with his hands and a lost dog was today's result. "Of course," said John, exasperated.

"Oh, jeez. Here, let me buy you another," the man offered.

"Thanks, but that's OK. I don't have much of an appetite anyway." John stood and checked his pants for errant condiments. He offered the man a nod.

"Have a nice day," the man called out, as John headed across the street.

Yeah, right, John thought.

* * *

"Please make yourself comfortable, Mr. Doyle. Dr. Mac should be in any minute," sang the peppy, young receptionist.

As John stepped toward the overstuffed chair closest to the door, his blood pressure rose slightly. Doctor? He still couldn't comprehend what he was in for. There was no name on the door or above the reception desk. The only signage was a bright, yellow happy face. It was a logo far too casual for the surroundings. The office gracing the seventh floor was intimidating—beautiful and well-appointed, yes, but too much so. Real work couldn't possibly be done in this office.

"Can I get you anything? Coffee? Water? A soda maybe?"

He was tempted to ask for a hot dog. "No thanks."

"All righty then," she chirped in a voice far too cheery for John's taste. He didn't trust people who put that much syrup in their voice.

Suddenly, the door swung open, and John cringed. In walked the man from the park bench. They recognized each other instantly.

"Well, isn't this a small world," the man said.

"You're Dr. Mac?" John asked.

"Mac Wilson. You can call me Mac." He extended a hand, which John took after a brief struggle getting himself out of the clutches of the chair.

"John Doyle."

John noticed immediately that Mac possessed the same indescribable presence that Walter had—larger than life. Mac was average in every physical way, but he somehow seemed taller, broader, and more distinguished.

Mac led John to his back office. No fluorescent tubes in here. Natural light flooded the large room from two walls of windows overlooking downtown. John scanned the office with equal parts envy and esteem. A large mahogany desk in front of a matching credenza supported a huge flat-screen computer monitor. All the signs of professional success were present and accounted for. On the one free wall, framed diplomas and certificates of achievement shared real estate with personal photos of happy, attractive people, grinning like they had all just won a game show. John stood near the door, arms crossed.

"You look worried," Mac said.

"No, I'm just... I gotta be honest. I have no idea what's going on or what— I mean, what is this, therapy?"

"Therapy? No. Definitely not therapy." Mac motioned to the black leather couch. "Would you care to lie down?"

John looked out toward the hall, planning his escape.

"I'm kidding," Mac assured, smiling broadly. "Why don't we get out of here. Let me buy you lunch. You must be starving."

"Seriously?"

"Truth is, I prefer to be out of this stuffy office as much as possible."

"You should see my office," John said.

"When your business is people, it makes more sense to be out with the people."

"So you're in the people business," John concluded, not quite realizing what he, himself, meant by it.

"Everyone is in the people business. Name me a line of work where people aren't involved."

John's mind immediately jumped to the challenge, as he racked his brain.

Mac smiled, as his question went unanswered.

* * *

Mac's pace never rose above a stroll, as he and John walked block after block on the crowded city streets. It made John anxious. He always walked with purpose. The way he saw it, if you were moving, you'd better leave a breeze in your wake.

"You married, John?"

"Fourteen years."

"Congratulations. That's success."

John shrugged. He hadn't thought of it that way, but after a day like yesterday, he welcomed any recognition of a win.

"And your work? Gail is your boss?"

John looked at him, surprised.

Mac noted the look and smiled, "I pay attention. My wife calls it being nosey. Comes with the territory, I guess."

"And what territory is that? What exactly is it you

do?"

"I do conflict," Mac replied.

"Sounds like a terrible job."

"If you judge the term by its stereotype, sure. But I define conflict by its potential, the potential to be prevented or its potential to be beneficial. If you see conflict as this big, ugly, five-headed beast, that's what conflict will always look like to you."

"But how do you *'do'* conflict?" John asked.

"Because I'm in control of it. I *do* conflict. It doesn't *do* me. I'm not a victim to it."

As John let that sink in, Mac abruptly turned into a small, quaint café. John could see why Mac liked the place. It opened out onto the street corner, and every table seemed to invite in the bustle of people going about their lives. They were seated at a table practically on the sidewalk.

"Sorry, Doc," John said. "What you're saying is interesting and all, but you still haven't answered my question. What do you do? For me?"

"What do you want to do?" Mac asked. He noticed the frustration welling up in John's face and continued, "Let me get right to the point for you..."

John wanted to say, *Finally!* Why couldn't the world communicate in bullet points?

"My work is built around understanding people," Mac said. "Whatever that may look like for an individual or an organization. I ask, 'What do you want to do?' and

I help them achieve it by exposing the people part of the equation. I help people master the ultimate skill."

"Soft skills."

"I see you pay attention, too." Mac nodded. "Soft skills—the hardest skills of them all. Something we're not formally taught growing up. We just make do."

"Barreling through life," said John.

"Like a bull in a china shop. The bull may get through the shop, but at what cost?"

John smiled grimly at the analogy. He'd always pictured himself as a bull. He liked the image—strong, formidable, an icon of success. Until now, he'd never connected the image to the china shop cliché.

"What is it costing you, John? Being the bull?"

John laughed—a shallow, self-effacing acknowledgement. He suddenly wanted to call up Walter Freeman and thank him for connecting him to this kooky guy with the funny logo.

"That's what I can do for you." Mac grinned, seeing in John's eyes the shift from suspicion to anticipation.

* * *

As the two men ate their late lunch, John recounted the events that had transpired the day before. He detailed his role at Starr Industries managing 10 sales reps, who sold Starr products across the state. He boasted about his crew almost always hitting their numbers and about the awards he had been given over the years. He was ready to move up the ladder—had been for the last two years. But twice now, he'd been passed over for a promotion—passed over by people who had less experience and weaker numbers.

"Sounds like you work hard—get the job done," Mac said.

"Work my tail off," John stated, proudly.

"Unfortunately for you, you're not working in a vacuum. Your approach seems to be piling up a bit of relationship carnage in its path."

"Look, Doc, sales is a tough business. Sometimes I drive my people pretty hard. I don't let the bean counters in the home office push me around either. I've been at Starr long enough to know what we need, so when I don't get it, I make some noise. It's like my dad used to say, 'Sometimes you've got to break a few eggs to make an omelet.'"

Mac grinned. "The omelets here are amazing, by the way."

John nodded, pretending to care.

Mac continued, "I remember you saying, 'Sales is all about people skills.' Clearly, you're a great salesperson. So, tell me about the people skills you use with potential customers."

"Well, you know... you get to know what they need. What they want. Figure out how to match that with what I have to sell."

"Exactly," said Mac.

"OK?" John felt he'd missed the point.

"That's an approach you've had success with, and I don't hear any eggshells breaking there," said Mac. He leaned in, locked eyes. "What if I could help you make your omelets without breaking nearly as many eggs? In other words, what if I could teach you how to manage conflict and build relationships in ways that lead to better results."

"Oh, I get the results," said John, defensively.

"You've hit your sales goals, true. But what about the other results you've been talking about? What about having a team of excited, motivated sales reps? What about that elusive promotion? I'm seeing a few too many eggshells on your floor."

John leaned back in his chair, sighed, "OK, fine. I'm sold."

"Ah! The seller becomes the sellee," joked Mac.

"What's this going to cost me?"

"Nothing."

"Come again?"

"It's taken care of," said Mac, flagging down the waitress.

"How is that possible?"

"Well, Walter Freeman seems to think an awful lot of you."

"He paid for me?"

Mac smiled warmly. "He and I have been working together long enough for him to see this as an investment.

I don't think he has a single executive in his organization that I haven't spent a little time with at some point."

John was overcome. He wasn't one of Walter's executives, he was just a vendor... a friend. John didn't have a whole lot of people he could call friends, and this act of selflessness made him regret that.

"This adventure is going to take some of that hard work of yours," Mac continued. "I'd like to meet five times over the next few weeks."

"In your office?"

"No, there are better ways of facilitating change than you and me staring at each other in my office. We'll mix it up."

"Where at?"

Mac laughed, "All right, John. I know you hate being in the dark, but work with me on this. I'll let you know. Just trust me."

"Trust?" John chuckled. "Guess the hard work is starting already."

"Give my assistant, Jenny, a call later this afternoon. She'll explain the inventories I'd like you to complete before we get back together. She'll also set up the appointment for our next rendezvous and give you the location."

John nodded and forced a smile to hide his apprehension.

"Ready to have a nice conflict?" asked Mac.

"Sure. I can't wait."

"You're lying, of course, but I appreciate your enthu-

siasm." Mac flashed a Cheshire cat smile and gave John a
playful slap on his back.

THREE

I CAN'T BELIEVE you have to work on a Saturday morning."

John's wife, Nancy, laid a plate of scrambled eggs in front of him, while he sat with their kids at the kitchen table.

"You have to work?" asked John, Jr., their 8-year-old son.

"It's not work, J.J.," explained John. "I have a doctor's appointment."

"Are you sick, Daddy?" asked 3-year-old Emma.

Nancy took her seat at the table between the two kids. She reached out and gave each of their arms a gentle squeeze. "No, Daddy's fine." She shot John a look.

He didn't need the scolding. He had already regretted his word choice. "It's a work doctor. I'm just getting some extra help."

"Like a tutor?" asked J.J.

"Yeah, I guess. Like a tutor."

Nancy frowned. "I just don't understand why it has to be on the weekend. You work hard enough as it is. The weekend is *our* time."

"I know it is," said John. "I'm just—"

He looked away, shaking his head, unable and unwilling to complete his thought. He still hadn't built up the nerve to admit to Nancy that he'd lost the promotion again. Now, the confession seemed inevitable.

"What's going on, hon?" asked Nancy.

John looked into her eyes and recognized her genuine concern. He couldn't ignore the soft urgency in her look. John shifted in his chair, "I had my meeting with HR."

She instantly put the pieces together—his distance, the sour mood. "I'm so sorry, John."

"What?" asked J.J.

John exhaled deeply. "I was hoping to get a new job at work, but it didn't happen."

"Why didn't you tell me?" asked Nancy, warmly.

John looked away. She stood and moved behind his chair, wrapping her arms around his neck in an embrace.

"It's going to be fine, honey," said Nancy. "It's just a dumb promotion. We'd love you if you were the janitor."

John stood, breaking Nancy's hug. "That's not the point, Nance. That promotion is important to me."

"I know it is. I just want you to know that we're here for you, no matter what. Starr Industries is just a job, you know."

"It's my life."

"It's a part of your life. Just like we're part of your life. A part I wish you'd remember a little more often," pleaded Nancy. "We care about you."

"I'm running late. I have to go," said John, taking his plate to the sink.

"Is this appointment of yours going to help you with your anger issues?"

"I don't have anger issues," replied John sharply, his tone countering his words. He retreated from the room, but Nancy trailed close behind.

"I'm just trying to help. I want you to be happy," said Nancy. "I'm just wondering if the anger may be contributing... to your struggles at your job."

John tried to silence her with a look. It didn't take.

Nancy continued, delicately. "I see you work so hard. I wonder if the stress of it all causes you, maybe, to rub people the wrong way."

"Well, who knows?" said John, roughly. "That's why I'm going. On a Saturday. Stealing our 'us' time."

"John—"

"I'm sorry. I'm just frustrated." John reached the door to the garage and turned to her. He saw the concern beaming from her eyes. It softened something within him. "I feel like there's so much I want to do with my life—so much I'm capable of. I've been told since high school I was a leader—that I can take charge of a situation and get people moving. That's what gets my blood pumping. But here I am, feeling like some dolt, stuck in the same job for four years, with my future looking more bleak every day."

"John, you know that I love you and want you to be happy. Got that?" She took him into a tight embrace.

"I know, honey. That's one thing I know for sure."

"You go see your conflict doctor, and we'll be here when you get home."

John gave Nancy a peck on the cheek and opened the door. She watched him from the doorway, as he opened his car door.

"And John? Have a nice conflict," she said with a wink.

* * *

"Turn right on Fairhaven; proceed to destination," said the female voice with a tinge of English accent. John welcomed the reminder from the GPS on his dashboard. He had spent most of the drive a million miles away—his mind awash with thoughts of his wife and family. Nancy had never understood the ambition that pulsed through his veins. It was like a foreign language to her. Sure, she had her interests. In fact, now that Emma was in pre-school, Nancy had started putting herself out there again, looking for freelance work. But it looked more like a hobby to John. Nancy was just missing the 'drive' he knew to be crucial to really succeed in the business world. Maybe if she understood that, she wouldn't make him feel so guilty about working so hard.

"Arriving at destination," said his dashboard.

John looked up at the sign in front of him: *Fairhaven Village Apartments. 1 & 2 Bedroom Units Available for Lease.* Could this be right? He checked the address against what was in the e-mail he had printed from Jenny, Dr. Mac's assistant. Everything appeared to match up.

The building looked more like a hotel circa 1940, with large, stone walls that had long since been painted over to keep up with the passing trends. At four stories tall, John guessed it housed around 50 apartments. The tall, ornate ironwork that separated the building's atrium from the street hinted at its past glory. Now, the dilapidated structure was likely home to struggling single moms, immigrant families, and a few college kids. He thought it unlikely that Mac called this place home. So what was he doing here? He repeated Mac's words to himself: *Just trust me.*

As John walked through the gate into the open-air center of the building, he could hear a baby's cry over the sounds of daytime television. The modest pool in the center was deserted, except for a small family of ducks. There was no sign of Dr. Mac. To his immediate right, John noticed a door labeled *Management Office.* He stepped inside the small, wood-paneled waiting room and was immediately assaulted by the smells of curry, cigarette smoke, and flowery perfume. He pressed the illuminated button next to a *Ring for Service* sign and waited.

After what felt like an eternity, a frosted glass window slid open. The sixty-something woman behind the glass was startling to behold in her heavy-handed make-up and orange, ruffled blouse. "Morning, sugar. Can I help you?" she asked.

"God, I hope so," John replied. "I'm supposed to meet a Mac Wilson here."

"Oh, you've come to the right place, Darlin'. Macky's my nephew. He's putzin' around in the boiler room, I think. Big metal door at the bottom of the stairs." She motioned to the stairwell door behind him.

John made his way down the dank, cement staircase. A muffled pounding could be heard echoing below. He couldn't help but question the doctor's sanity. Then again, maybe he should be questioning his own sanity for going along with this. He tried to imagine Walter Freeman descending these stairs. Would the old titan of industry have been forced to knock on this giant, rusty door like a thirsty laborer trying to get in to some secret speakeasy?

But here it was, his turn. The ominous door looked too substantial for a simple knuckle knock, so he used the edge of a quarter which made a distinct clicking sound, one he hoped could be heard over the hammering and music coming from within.

After several taps, the hammering stopped, and the

Mac looked around. "I guess you're right. I've spent so many years in this workshop, I don't even think about it. When my grandpa ran the place, I was here helping him out after school, on weekends, during summer breaks—I practically grew up here from middle school, all the way through grad school."

As Mac spoke, he screwed a pipe-fitting onto a long, flat appliance he had resting across two sawhorses. John didn't recognize it and couldn't make out any of the labeling on the cardboard box and packing materials littering the floor. Mac went to one end and motioned to the other, "Can you grab the other side? I need to flip this over."

John followed orders.

"Thanks."

John gave up trying to identify the appliance. He was more interested in finding out why he was in the bowels of some crumbling, old building. He crossed his arms and leaned roughly against the cluttered workbench. Mac eyed him and put down the instruction manual he was flipping through.

"A lot of what I know about conflict I learned right here in this building," said Mac.

"Oh, yeah? How's that?"

Mac motioned around him, "It's a virtual petri dish of conflict."

John pulled away from the workbench.

"Don't worry. You won't get any on you," laughed

"Yeah? What is it?"

"Tankless water heater. I'm installing them in each of the units to replace the boiler. The old girl needs a lot of work. Expensive work. And after years of complaints about not enough hot water, I figured out I can modernize the system in a way that makes everyone happy and pays for itself in the long run. Conflict can be an opportunity to step back and assess the situation—find creative solutions."

"So, how come your grandfather never reinforced the walls?"

"He wanted to. He just got too old to take on the project. And by that time, I was making my way in the business world."

"So he just took the complaints for all those years?"

"He did. But it was never a problem for him. He was a master conflict manager. His tenants loved him. He just knew how to deal with it."

"And how was that?" asked John, praying for a silver bullet answer.

Mac smiled. "Well, that depends."

John slumped back. "You're killing me, Doc."

"Seriously. It's an important point, John. The answer is, 'It depends.' There's no one-size-fits-all answer," explained Mac. "The way he'd deal with apartment 3-B would be completely different from how he'd deal with 4-A or 2-F."

"Let me guess. Back to people skills," said John.

"Turns out the skill that made him a successful bank manager for three decades was the most important skill he needed as the landlord here. It takes the ability to work well with people—to help people feel worthwhile and meet them where they're at. It's the only way you're ever going to influence them. He made it a point to build relationships wherever he could and taught me to do the same."

Mac wiped his hands on a rag and moved toward the doorway. "Check this out," he said, as he walked out, disappearing into the boiler room.

John found Mac standing in front of the big metal door, looking at the large plaque that hung above it. In hand-carved letters, it read: *The most important single ingredient in the formula of success is knowing how to get along with people." —Theodore Roosevelt*

"Every time my grandpa would leave to interact with the people upstairs, this would serve as a reminder," said Mac with a flash of melancholy. Mac was surrounded by traces of his grandfather, but this plaque appeared to be the most significant to him.

John sensed the emotional moment but didn't quite know what to do with it. "Good stuff," was all he could come up with.

Mac smiled, still staring at the plaque. "I think so. Teddy Roosevelt was his favorite U.S. president. He read books about him, had a big, framed photo on the wall next to his desk. He quoted the guy all the time. But this quote was most meaningful to him. This was the one he drilled into me all those summers and weekends growing up."

Mac finally looked at John, waiting for him to make eye contact. "You see, my Grandpa knew that it took a lot more than being good at one's job to achieve success."

Mac returned to his workshop, letting those words sink in. John recalled the countless times he had bragged about his skills as a salesman—to himself and to others. It had served as a 'get out of jail free' card for him for years. How many times had people at work let him get away with his rougher edges because he was a star salesman? John frowned. Whatever the number, it was clear to him that being the star had lost much of its cachet over the past few years. He missed it. He wanted the feeling back. And if hanging out in a 70-year-old basement with Dr. Mötley Crüe on a Saturday morning was going to help him regain a little shine, then so be it.

John found Mac back at work on the water heater. "OK, so it's all about getting along with people," said John. "Sounds easier said than done. Or is it just me who's banging my head against a wall?"

"No. You're not alone, John. Working with people can be tricky. Even for me. My grandfather was the best I've ever seen, and even he struggled. Of course, here he could just evict the person," said Mac with a wink.

"Hard to evict a wife or a boss," said John.

"True. That's why it's important to always be working to get better at dealing with people. Getting along with people is not always easy, but I can help make it a whole lot easier than it is now."

"Wish it didn't have to be so frustrating," said John.

"Why do you suppose it is, John?"

"Cause most people are insane," laughed John.

Mac didn't mirror John's smile. "Seriously. Why do you think people are so hard to understand?"

John thought a second. "Because we have no idea what's going on inside their head."

Mac smiled broadly. "Precisely." He held up the instruction manual for the tankless water heater. "You know, it's funny—whenever you buy anything new, it almost always comes with an owner's manual. Yet with people—who are much more complicated and dynamic than any piece of equipment—we've got to figure them out on our own. We don't get an owner's manual for our relationships."

"That's what you need to make. An instruction manual for people," said John.

"Well, in a way it already exists. Remember those assessments I had you take?"

"Then what are we supposed to do to figure people out? Make them take an assessment?" asked John.

"That would be nice, but no. The key is trying to identify *why* people do what they do. The challenge is, most of what we have to go on involves watching *what* they do. We can see their behavior, but it's more worthwhile to understand their reason for using the behavior—their intent or motivation. Take the behavior of 'Ambition.' I know this is something you find important. But *why* is it important to you?"

"Ambition? It just is. Always has been," replied John.

"OK, good to note. But think about it. What is it about being ambitious that appeals to you?"

John thought for a moment, "I like the feeling of being the best at something. I like having a goal and then beating it. I guess ambition helps push me to get those things."

"Perfect. So for you, the use of ambition as a behavior helps you to fulfill your motivation of being the best and achieving your goals."

"I suppose so, yeah."

"So let's look at another example of ambition. Do you remember General Norman Schwarzkopf?"

"Sure. Stormin' Norman," John said.

"Best known American general since World War II. Known to be aggressive, direct, and confrontational. But those are behaviors. His motivation might surprise you. While you may use ambition to be the best and reach your goals, Schwarzkopf used ambition for entirely different reasons. Did you know he was so disgruntled with the state of the Army after Vietnam, he almost left? But after much soul-searching, he realized he needed to stay. He realized that if he moved up the ranks, he could help the Army and restore its reputation in the eyes of the

American public. The guy was tough but caring—always thinking about the welfare of his troops. Schwarzkopf used ambition in support of others."

"So what are you saying? My ambition is selfish?"

"Not at all," said Mac. "I'm just making the distinction that ambition is a behavior. It's a tool that both of you use effectively. But you're using it for different reasons."

Mac went to a battered metal tool chest that stood nearly five feet tall. He slid out the top drawer and removed a large, flat-head screwdriver. "Take this screwdriver. One tool, but I use it to open paint cans and turn screws. I even use it as a chisel in a pinch. One tool—several different motivations for using it. So in the case of people, we can look at their behavior, but it's not the whole story, is it?"

"You can't judge a book by its behavior," said John.

"Precisely," said Mac. "Behaviors are the tools we choose and use to support our self-worth."

"What do you mean by 'self-worth?'"

"Our underlying motivation or set of values. Those things which make us feel good about ourselves and make us feel like we're contributing."

"And I feel good about myself when I'm getting things done and excelling and being in charge," offered John.

"So you most often will pick the tool that you feel will be most successful at getting you those feelings."

"Makes sense," said John, as he took a seat on a creaky stool.

"Excellent. So let's look at the results of one of the assessments I had you complete." Mac poked around his messy workshop, looking under cardboard scraps until he found his shiny, black briefcase hidden under a pile of bubble-wrap. From inside, he removed a paper. "Remember this?"

John instantly recognized the diamond-shaped pattern of squares. "Sure. That was my ranking of strengths, right?"

"For the sake of this conversation, you can look at personal strengths like behaviors. They represent the different ways a person can interact with others to achieve self-worth. When a person tries one of these strengths and has success with it, they use it more often. Other strengths might have rendered poor results, and so they might tend to use those less and less. Over time, we develop a set of 'go-to' strengths. They become our modus operandi."

"OK. So what's my M.O.?" asked John, with a mischievous grin.

"Well, based on the way you prioritized your strengths, you are probably most comfortable operating in the realm of *self-confidence, competitiveness*, and, of course, there's our old friend, *ambition*. You also like to be *fair, quick to act,* and *principled*."

"Are those good?" asked John.

"All of the strengths are valuable, so it's not a question of whether they are good or bad," replied Mac. "These are the strengths you identified as being most like you and therefore, the ones you use often to enhance your sense of self-worth. You're most likely to rely on these top six because you're most comfortable with them in your interactions with others."

"I'd say that's true," said John.

"Now down here at the bottom of your chart you placed *cautious, tolerant, caring, socializer, adaptable,* and *experimenter*. I would venture to guess that it can be difficult for you to use those strengths and not much fun when you feel like you have to."

"Horrible," replied John. "What about all those strengths in the middle? Those were kinda tough to differentiate."

"That would make sense. We all have a good sense for the strengths we're most comfortable with and those that are most unlike us, but the strengths in the middle... they actually offer the greatest opportunities."

"Opportunities? How do you figure?" asked John.

"Let me ask you a fundamental question, John," said Mac, as he sat on the stool next to John. "Do you believe we choose our own behavior?"

John thought for a moment, "I guess. Sure."

"OK. Let's make the question a little tougher," continued Mac. "Do you believe that you *always* have the ability to choose your behavior?"

"I don't know. I know it doesn't always feel as if I have a lot of choices."

Mac studied him for a minute, his wheels turning. He then hopped off his stool and held up the screwdriver, "Remember our tool analogy..."

"Behaviors are like tools," said John.

"Right!" Mac tapped the tool chest with the handle. "So let's say this old tool chest represents me and all the behaviors or strengths I have to work with."

"Gee, Mac. You could use a coat of paint," said John.

Mac smiled. "What? And cover up all this charm? I've had this thing for 30 years." He gave the giant tool chest a loving pat on the side.

"So in the top drawers of this beauty," continued Mac, "I keep the tools I use most—screwdrivers, pliers, adjustable wrenches, and my two favorite hammers." Mac opened and closed the top two metal drawers. "They're all here, right at eye level. Easy to get at and I use them often."

Mac opened a lid on the very top of the chest and pulled out a leather tool belt stocked with tools, "In fact, I even have my tool belt that I keep with me anytime I'm working on a project upstairs. The tools in here are like my top strengths—they're always with me. Think back to your top three strengths: *self-confident, competitive,* and *ambitious*. I bet those feel like they're right in your back pocket—ready to whip out at a moment's notice."

"Absolutely," agreed John.

Mac returned the tool belt and continued, "The tools I use less frequently are in these middle drawers... wrench and socket sets, crowbar, screen repair tools, and everything related to working with electricity are all here in the middle. I can use these tools when I need them, but I'm just not as confident with them as some of the others."

Mac squatted down and slid open the bottom two drawers, "I keep the tools I use the least here in the bottom. For the most part, they're all of my plumbing tools and supplies. I hate to do plumbing, and I'm not good at it. In fact, I've made quite a few messes over the years, trying to do plumbing projects. It's just not something I'm comfortable with."

"So those are like your bottom strengths," said John.

"Exactly," said Mac. He stood and kicked the bottom drawers closed.

"So what does your toolbox have to do with choosing behaviors?" asked John.

"Do you see any locks on that chest?"

"No."

"So no matter what I'm faced with, I have the ability to choose the right tool for the job," said Mac, returning to his stool. "Let's say I get a call from a tenant that has a repair problem. The quickest, easiest thing to do would be to grab my tool belt and run upstairs. But if I don't know what I'm dealing with, I may be unprepared to deal with the real issue. And if I go ahead and force myself to use whatever I happen to have in my tool belt, it may take me twice as long to fix the problem. Worse yet, I may do some damage."

"So you're saying if I go into every situation using my top strengths every time, I'm causing conflict?" said John.

"Your 'go-to' strengths will serve you well. After all, you wouldn't keep using them if they didn't work for you. But it's important to remember that you have a whole tool chest of other options that may get you better results from time to time," Mac grabbed John's strength chart again and pointed to the center area. "All these strengths here in the center of your list—all these tools in your middle drawers—you don't hate using these. They're OK. These are your best opportunities to take on a situation or a relationship a little more prepared—with a little more deliberate choice."

"Sounds like work," groaned John.

"I thought you liked a challenge."

"I do. But I also like to get things done quickly."

"Does using a strength that's easy for you but ends up damaging a relationship with an important person in your life help you reach your goals quicker?"

John felt that question tear right through him.

"And the fact is," Mac continued. "It doesn't have to be challenging or time-consuming. Like anything else, once you know how to do it and what to look for, it becomes second nature. You start to see people—not by what they do on the outside, but by what you know is important to them. By what you know gives them their own self-worth. People are most effective when they choose a strength that enhances the self-worth of others while helping them achieve their own goals—their own self-worth.

"Sounds like a 'win-win,'" said John.

"Sounds like a productive, rewarding relationship," said Mac in agreement. "I'm guessing you like being in charge, John."

"Of course. Who doesn't?"

Mac made a pained face. John instantly understood his error. Seeing the world from another person's perspective was going to take some effort.

"Sorry," said John. "What I meant to say was, 'Yes, I, personally, love being in charge.'"

"That's what I thought you said," said Mac with a smile. "All I'm asking you to do is take control—be in charge of your behavior. When you act in whatever way feels easy or convenient, you're not taking charge of your actions. When you choose a behavior that's right for the situation and the person you're with, you're in control of yourself. You're running the show."

John laughed, "You sure know how to pull all my right levers."

"I'm just speaking your language—by knowing what's important to you."

"So where's the line between speaking my language

and manipulation?" asked John with a sly grin.

"Is the way I'm communicating with you making sense to you? Am I getting through to you and giving you what you want from our time together?"

"Absolutely."

"Then I've achieved each of our goals by choosing behavior that works for both of us. It's win-win, right?" asked Mac. "If I was in Japan and I knew how to speak Japanese, shouldn't I do so? Wouldn't I get better results? Is that manipulation?"

"No."

"Not at all. It's respect if it's anything," said Mac. "When we choose, we get to be in control of our outcomes."

"What if you choose the wrong behavior?" asked John.

"It's going to happen, sure. And there are consequences that come with the choices we make. With choice comes responsibility and accountability. When we choose to act a certain way, we also choose the result that comes from doing so. But more importantly, we're influencing what happens in our relationships, so we can be more in control of our lives and our careers, which, I think, is why we're working together."

John nodded, letting Mac's words sink in. He thought about his mother, which he seldom did when facing issues in the world. It was always his father's gems of old-world wisdom that rattled around in his head, branded on his brain. "It's funny," said John, finally. "Growing up, my mother always used to say the same thing to me every time I left the house: 'Make good choices, son.'"

"Smart lady," said Mac with a smile. "If we make good choices, we are more likely to have good outcomes. Poor choices—or worse, *no* choices—make us more likely to get poor results in our relationships, and that usually means we're not getting what we want."

Just then, the old rotary phone hanging on the wall shrieked loudly. It caused John to jump a little.

"Sorry about that. Had to make the ringer power tool proof." Mac answered. "Hello, Dolly. What's up?" As he listened, his smile dissolved. "No, don't do anything. I'll be right up." He hung up the phone and turned to John. "I have a tenant complaint to deal with."

"What? A noise complaint?" kidded John.

"Yes, actually."

"So much for extra drywall."

"Want to join me?" asked Mac.

"Why? Do you need backup?"

John was joking, but Mac didn't return the smile. He was already on the move. John wondered if Mac was busy packing his mental tool belt.

* * *

"I'm calling the damn cops." The phrase seemed out-of-place coming from the short, frail, elderly woman Mac introduced as Mabel Grimes. John guessed she was in her

90s but she looked to have the energy of a woman half her age.

Mac sat down with her in the lobby of the management office. "Mabel, tell me what the problem is."

John tried to look inconspicuous lurking in the doorway.

"It's that hoodlum from next door," snapped Mabel. "I swear, he's trying to make me go deaf with that horrible noise."

"Kraig playing his guitar again?" Mac looked over at Dolly, who watched from the sliding window smoking a cigarette. They shared a frown.

Mabel sighed dramatically, "I travelled all through the night and I don't think it's too much to expect some peace and quite when I get into my own home."

"Not at all, Mabel. I completely understand why you're upset; I'll deal with it right away." With that, Mac stood. "OK?"

"Thank you, Theodore," said Mabel.

Two minutes later, John was following Mac up a creaky staircase. As they passed the Level 2 door, John couldn't hold it back any longer, "Theodore?"

"What do you want?" said Mac, "She's ninety-two."

"So what's the story with this Kraig guy?" asked John.

"Kraig Gannon. 3-F. He's a really nice kid. But he has an unfortunate hobby of being in a heavy metal band. He's actually a pretty talented guitar player and songwriter, but it's not exactly Miss Mabel's cup of tea. She's the Fairhaven's longest-running tenant. My Grandpa rented to her in 1979, when she was still teaching middle school."

They reached the third floor fire door and stepped into the hall. Instantly, John could hear the muffled guitar licks blaring. Mac was right; Kraig was good—but loud.

Standing in front of Apartment 3-F, Mac knocked. The music continued. After a moment, Mac knocked again, this time more loudly. Still the guitar sang with hyperactive intensity. From his back pocket, Mac produced the big flathead screwdriver, held it up to John with a conspiratory smile. He banged on the door with the handle end. "Hey, Kraig, it's Mac. Open up."

The guitar stopped, and the apartment door swung open. The 20-something man that filled the doorway glistened with piercings. Tattoos covered his torso like graffiti on an old New York subway car. It took a moment for John to realize he was only wearing his boxers and socks. Kraig smiled broadly, "Heyyy! What's crackin' Mac daddy? I see you're rockin' the Crüe shirt today."

"Of course," said Mac. "Kraig, this is my friend, John Doyle."

"Hey, what's up, man?" said Kraig, warmly, as they shook hands.

"Hi," said John.

John laughed to himself. He was not expecting this mutant with the scraggly black hair to be so friendly.

"Can we come in for a minute?" asked Mac.

"Sure, man. Can I get you guys a beer?"

"No thanks," Mac said, as he and John stepped inside Kraig's apartment. The threadbare pink and gold plaid sofa was winning the fight against the faded orange stripes of the recliner. A small television balanced precariously on a stool below a framed poster of AC/DC's Angus Young, in full concert strut. In the corner, a 5-foot high Marshall speaker stack still hissed. Kraig returned his Union Jack-painted electric guitar to its stand and disappeared around the corner, "Make yourself at home," he called out.

"Sounding good, Kraig. How's the band?"

"Yeah, man! Killer news. We just got that festival gig I was tellin' you about," Kraig reappeared, beer in hand. "Can you believe it? Ten-thousand screaming idiots have the chance to consume our tasty tunage."

Kraig fell into his couch and dropped his feet on the makeshift coffee table—a weathered old door stretched across cinder blocks.

"That's great news, Kraig. I know how hard you've worked for that band of yours. That's going to be great for you guys," said Mac, showing genuine excitement.

"We're so fired up."

"Unfortunately, Ms. Grimes would rather skip the pre-show," said Mac.

"What?" asked Kraig dumbfounded.

Mac nodded to the speakers. "I know you don't mean

any harm, but we've talked about this before. You've gotta keep it down or use your headphones. You're gonna give Miss Grimes a heart attack."

"Dude, I'm so sorry. I had no idea Able Mabel was back in town. I guess I got carried away after hearing the news—broke out into my own private concert. Honestly, man. I thought she was still visiting her grandkids in Chicago."

"Well, she's back. And the noise is really bothering her."

"Oh, man," said Kraig running his fingers nervously through his wild black hair. "She must be steaming. I'll go talk to her. I should go talk to her, right?"

"That'll be fine, Kraig, but, hey... Put a shirt and pants on before you go over," said Mac with a wink.

Kraig looked down, realized what he was wearing. "Of course. You got it, boss man." Kraig stood, gave Mac a soul-style handshake and a shoulder-to-shoulder half embrace. "Thanks for the heads-up. I'll keep it on the D.L. the rest of the day. We've got rehearsal in an hour anyway."

"Thanks for understanding. And hey, congrats on the festival," said Mac as they stepped back into the hallway.

As John and Mac entered the stairwell and made their way back down, John said, "Well, that was tame."

"Sorry to disappoint. You were expecting blood and guts?"

"A little, yeah," said John with a smile.

"Having a nice conflict takes some guts, but no blood. You're going to have to stop seeing conflict as a battle, if our time together is going to be productive at all."

"I know," said John with a nod. "But could you even call what just happened conflict?"

"It was if you consider how those conversations could have gone. What you saw was conflict nipped in the bud before it escalated into something ugly. Mabel certainly was in conflict. She's normally a very patient, soft-spoken woman."

"She looked like a firecracker to me."

"Cause she was in conflict. Her self-worth was being threatened. And to Mabel Grimes, that looks like someone ready to put on the gloves and jump in the ring. My job was to keep a misunderstanding from becoming an unsalvageable war between two people who need to co-exist. Every tenant is an important relationship to me—personally and financially. It is in my best interest and theirs to maintain a positive relationship. The goal wasn't about winning a battle. It was about bringing everyone back to a state of feeling good—maintaining their self-worth."

"So how'd you do it?" asked John.

"You tell me."

"I don't know."

"Well, what did you notice?" asked Mac.

John replayed the two interactions he had just witnessed in his mind. "You were different with each of them," said John.

"OK. How so?"

"With Mabel, you just listened and promised to handle it right away. And then with Kraig, you kinda hung out and chatted about his music, before dropping the hammer."

"Two different people. Two different approaches," said Mac. "And in the end, all three of us are satisfied. And as for you, if you want blood and guts, rent a movie."

Mac slapped John on the shoulder, as he opened the stairwell door for him.

* * *

Mac walked John back to John's car in the bright mid-day sun. John was glad their meeting hadn't gone too late. He was still conscious of his family's disappointment that morning. He really hadn't been present for them for the past few weeks—maybe longer—and needing to "work" on a Saturday wasn't helping. Now it looked as if part of the day would be salvageable.

"Do you understand your homework?" asked Mac, as John dug in his pocket for his keys.

"I think so. Get feedback from a few people about some of my top strengths," answered John.

"Right. Now, John, it's important that people feel comfortable enough to truly be honest about this. You want a true assessment, and it's up to you to create that space of trust and honesty. Feedback is a gift. All you need to offer in return is your thanks. Try not to be defensive or offer any explanations."

"The only thing I don't understand is the negative part. If these are my strengths, why am I asking for examples where they felt they were negative?" asked John.

"Well, remember what we talked about? Oftentimes, we try to use strengths that aren't suitable for the situation. If I have a screw to tighten, I'm going to cause damage if all I brought was my hammer. We're looking for feedback from both sides of the coin. We want to know when a particular strength was seen as a positive and times when that strength became a negative."

"So like when my *self-confidence* was misused?"

"Precisely. And sometimes, a personal strength can cause conflict when it's *overdone*," said Mac.

"What do you mean 'overdone?'" asked John.

"It's like our friend upstairs, Kraig. Our strengths may sound like beautiful music to us, but they can come across as too loud or overdone to others, like Mabel. Kraig's guitar would have sounded just as good to him in his headphones, but he chose to turn up the volume and let it fly."

John sighed, starting to feel deflated. He moved to the back of his car and leaned against the trunk. "So you're saying my *strengths* are the cause of all my problems?"

"Look John, I'm not saying your strengths are the problem. But it's important to know which strengths we favor and understand that those strengths, when overdone or misapplied, can become weaknesses."

Mac joined him by the trunk of John's car and continued, "Let's look at *self-confidence*. What would that look like to people if it was overdone—if the volume was too high?"

"Cocky?"

"Sure. Cocky, arrogant. It's not your intent, of course. But is it possible that some of your conflict at work happens because other people don't see your strengths the way you intend them to be seen? Self-confidence is at the top of your list of strengths. Do you think you ever turn up the volume too much on that?"

John smiled grimly. "Some of the people in the office probably think I've got my volume jacked up to 11." John thought about the times when he had been accused of being a little too proud—too sure of himself—his standard rebuttal had always been: "It ain't braggin' if I can do it." He thought about all the people at work who may be misinterpreting his behavior and seeing the overdone versions. "So what about my other strengths. What would those look like?"

"Well let's think about them. What would *competitive* be if taken too far?" asked Mac.

John thought for a moment. He found it hard to separate his intention from another person's perception of it. "Maybe aggressive or combative?"

"Sure," said Mac. "What about *ambitious* or *quick to act?*"

"I guess those could be seen as ruthless and rash. And *principled* could be seen as stubborn, maybe, or unyielding. What about *fair?*" asked John.

"Well, fair is about being impartial and equitable. When overdone, that can start to look cold and unfeeling," said Mac.

John let the list of negative words roll around in his head. He had often struggled to understand why people always seemed to misinterpret his good intentions. Now, the issue was crystallizing in his head, and the jagged points were hurting his brain. When he saw himself as "ambitious" others might be seeing the same thing as "ruthless." How many "Miss Mabels" had come down to HR to complain about his volume levels at work? How many people on his team saw him as stubborn or rash? How many of them were simply tolerating him or avoiding him altogether?

"Wow, Doc," sighed John. "When you look at it like that, it's no wonder I turn so many people off."

Mac smiled warmly. "Don't get down on yourself, John. The good news about overdone strengths is all they require are gaining more volume control over the positive strengths you already have. It's not some weakness you have to rid yourself of. People are almost always trying to do good, and they're usually seeking feelings of self-worth. It's true for you, which means it's true for others too."

"So when I find another person's behavior annoying..."

"Look for the strength behind it. What are they overdoing? What are they really trying to accomplish? Most likely, their intent is not to annoy you. If you can find the strength lurking behind the perceived weakness, you've discovered insight into that person that may help you understand them better—preventing potential conflict by avoiding misperceptions of their behavior."

"Wow," said John, letting this realization soak in. He hated to admit that he found most people's behavior annoying—almost to the point of doubting himself. He'd often thought maybe his expectations were too high or he just lacked patience for people. But now, he was faced with an alternate explanation. When he felt impatience with his boss, Gail's, tendency to nitpick or when he felt smothered by his wife's attention, perhaps he needed to look behind those things and understand their intent.

Mac stepped away from the car. "All it takes is insight and practice and the realization that you have a choice—and that's why we're working together, right?"

John offered his hand and a smile, "That we are."

Mac took his hand, and they shook, "Enjoy the rest of your weekend. And don't forget to do your homework."

"Yes, professor," said John, frowning. "I can't wait."

FOUR

WHAT THE HELL was he thinking? John hesitated just outside the doorway to Gail's office. He was second-guessing his decision to start this feedback process with her. The truth was, he hadn't been thinking at all, and now, the inertia of his decision was propelling him into her office, feeling unprepared.

It was at that moment that Gail rushed out of her office and nearly ran into him. It took both of them by surprise.

"Oh!" she yelped. It may have been the first time John had witnessed an emotion out of her. She regained her composure, "John. What—"

"Hey. I uhh— I was just coming to see you,"

"I'm afraid I'm neck-deep in it right now. I'm working to get everything in order for that meeting with operations this afternoon."

"That's fine. We can talk later. I just needed to get

some information from you," said John, feeling relieved.

Gail was intrigued by John's uncharacteristic awkwardness. She studied him over her frameless glasses, "I was going to grab a quick bite down at the commissary. Would you want to join me?"

"The commissary?" asked John, surprised. The building's eatery had been dubbed a "last resort" by most who had the misfortune of eating there. "Sure, why not? Let's live dangerously."

* * *

John paid the commissary cashier and found Gail at a corner table near the windows. He marveled at the simple green salad before her. In the years he'd worked with her, he'd never seen her eat anything else. After consuming two cherry tomatoes from her plate, she eyed him. "What did you want to discuss?"

"Me, actually."

Gail's head cocked slightly.

"I got myself involved in something that I'm pretty sure is going to help me out around here," said John.

Gail raised an eyebrow. "Should I be worried?"

"What? No," said John. "I'm seeing a guy about helping me be a better manager and deal with people better—manage conflict better."

"Oh," she said, surprised. "Well, that's magnificent, John."

There she was, showing emotion again. "Yeah, it's

pretty eye-opening stuff."

"For example?" Gail prodded.

"Well," said John, searching for a good sound bite from Saturday, "for example, he talks about how people don't really have weaknesses so much as they have strengths that they may use at the wrong time or use too intensely. He calls them overdone strengths. And they can be a big source of conflict between people."

"That's intriguing. I've never thought of it quite like that. Did he give you anything? Any support material?"

"Not yet. I completed a couple of assessments, but we haven't really gone through them in detail yet. All I know is it's a concept of Relationship Awareness Theory."

"Huh," said Gail, intrigued.

"So this guy I'm working with gave me some homework to do."

"Really," said Gail with a hint of a smile. "I'm beginning to like him already."

John had forgotten that Gail was an adjunct professor at a local university. She taught a course on market research or statistics or something like that. He figured the whole idea of homework must have a certain sadistic appeal to her.

"Well I can't do your homework for you, John," said Gail. "I haven't done that since high school."

"No, of course not," said John. "I just need to collect a little feedback from you."

"I'm not sure what I'll be able to offer you, given everything I still need to prepare for today. If I can't give you what you need right now, can I get back to you after I've had a chance to give it some thought?"

John bit his lip and smiled, "Of course." All John wanted was some simple, off-the-cuff impressions, but Gail seemed incapable of speaking off the top of her head. Her acute analysis paralysis had always been an irritation to John. As he felt himself feeling annoyed, he remembered Mac's advice. He recognized this as one of those opportunities to look beneath her tendency to be anal and find the underlying strength. When he really thought about it, he had always truly respected Gail's experience and expertise. Her analytical approach and thirst for detail had saved his butt on more than one occasion.

John glanced at his notes and pushed on. "So, one of the things we worked on was determining my top six personal strengths. What I identified for myself includes self-confident, competitive, ambitious, fair, quick to act, and principled. What do you think?"

John looked up at Gail and waited for a reaction. She paused for what seemed to be an eternity. "I would probably agree with that assessment. But can I be honest?"

"Absolutely. I need you be honest," said John, who flashed a wry smile and continued, "at least as honest as you were on my performance appraisal."

"Would you like this feedback or not?" she asked, not amused.

"Sorry."

"Are you sure 'quick to act' is a strength? In my book, this need of yours to move so quickly on everything has gotten you in some trouble over the years."

"Well, that's what I'm after," said John. "I need to know how some of these traits might be working against me at times. Do you have an example?"

"OK. Let me think for a minute." Gail squeezed a wedge of lemon into her iced tea, stirred it slowly and set the spoon squarely in the center of a paper napkin. John watched the ritual with newfound curiosity.

"EagleMark," said Gail, finally.

John winced. He knew what was coming next. She had rubbed his nose in the EagleMark fiasco many times over the past year. Why not now?

"You barged into my office to push me on discounting for EagleMark Enterprises. You had just come from your lunch meeting with Mr. Willis, and you had yourself convinced that the account was—let me see if I can recall your exact words— *'This guy is a whale in waiting. I can turn EagleMark into our biggest volume customer in one year.'* You perched yourself in front of my desk and badgered me until I finally gave in."

John's face burned. He stared at his notepad fighting the urge to fight his side.

"And where is your whale now?" continued Gail. "If I recall the last year-to-date report correctly, EagleMark is in the bottom 10% of all active accounts in the country, *and* they're receiving our deepest discount." Gail took a sip of iced tea, as if to quell a potential flare-up. "I'm still taking heat for that, and I sure hope it doesn't come up today in my meeting upstairs."

John shifted in his chair. "I believe you called it 'irrational exuberance.' At least that's what I remember from my performance appraisal."

"My exact words," said Gail, with a bit of satisfaction. Being accurately quoted had always been a big deal for her. Misquoting her or taking her words out of context were well-known ways to find yourself on Gail's bad side.

John's mind was swelling with explanations and excuses about the EagleMark situation. He hadn't thought about how hard it was going to be to just listen to the feedback without comment. He eked out a simple, "OK."

"Whether that account had been successful or not, I didn't appreciate your approach with me at all." Gail took a bite of salad—a clear signal that the topic would no longer be discussed. She hated bringing it up almost as much as John hated being reminded. The EagleMark situation had been a frequent weapon used against both of them by the executives upstairs.

John was happy to change the subject and possibly end on a positive note. "Are there times when my strengths have really benefited the organization?" asked John hopefully.

"Sure, John. I think you bring a lot to my team— your competitive drive, desire to succeed, and high level of confidence can raise the bar for everyone—especially when you and Randy start trying to outdo each other in sales contests. It gets everyone engaged and causes all of us to think more about our business. I also know that when you really believe in something, you don't let anything stand in your way. I look at an account like Hemisphere Worldwide... We wouldn't be where we are today with them if you hadn't seen the opportunity that was beneath the surface."

"See. Sometimes I know what I'm talking about." said John with a sheepish grin.

"But in the case of Hemisphere, you did your research first and came to me with a game plan. You weren't so impulsive."

"Thanks, Gail. I'm glad you appreciate the work I put into that one."

"I do appreciate it, John. And I appreciate you and the work you're doing with this consultant. I truly think you've got potential to do great things in this company, but you've got some work to do on the people front. Your approach doesn't sit well with everyone." Gail glanced at her watch and started collecting her utensils in a neat pile on her plate. "I need to head back upstairs."

"Thanks for your input, Gail. I'm trying."

"I see that. I think it's wonderful what you're doing. Keep me informed about your progress."

What he saw in Gail's face wasn't a smile, but there was a subtle pride in her eyes that he hadn't seen in a long time.

As he watched her leave, his thoughts swirled as he recounted the conversation. He picked up his pen to write some notes.

"Hey, John-John. Can I join you?"

John looked up and saw Leslie from marketing. Without waiting for an answer, she slid into what had been Gail's chair. Leslie was Starr Industries' "town crier." There wasn't a rumor in the building she hadn't heard or started. John had no doubt Leslie had been watching his lunch with Gail from afar and was bursting with curiosity. He scanned the room for an escape route.

"What's going on?" asked Leslie. "I heard about the regional position. I'm so sorry."

"Well, that's the way it goes sometimes," said John. He had no interest in opening up to her about how he was really feeling. He was mortified enough, knowing she knew about it. Then again, if anyone would...

"I'd be pissed. Who else are they going to give it to, Randy? Guy's the world's biggest exaggerator."

John smiled to himself at the irony of calling someone the world's biggest exaggerator. He took his first bite of his dried out club sandwich—anything to not have to engage her on a subject that was still so tender. Leslie seemed unfazed by John's detachment from the conversation. He hoped he wasn't the only one who found Leslie exhausting.

"Did Gail beat you up today?" asked Leslie. "I bet

she dredged up the EagleMark thing again."

John looked up from his sandwich. "I swear, Leslie, you must have this building bugged."

"She did, didn't she?" asked Leslie. John's look gave her the answer. "Look, John, we're on the same team on that one. I thought EagleMark would be a winner, too. And believe me, I got my 40 lashes over it going flop as well."

"Yeah," John conceded sourly. "Guess you should be leery next time I start waving a flag around."

"No way, John. We need your kind of energy around here. EagleMark may have been a dud, but there are five more just like it that you called perfectly. I love working with you on stuff."

John looked her in the eye for the first time. He had no idea she felt that way. He knew Leslie had taken some heat, and he felt largely responsible for that. The guilt reminded him of his homework assignment. He hadn't planned on using Leslie as a feedback provider, but he couldn't resist the opportunity to knock two out in one lunch.

"So, Les?" John asked with a hint of collusion. "We've known each other, what—almost three years now, right?"

"No, I'm not running away with you, John Doyle," said Leslie, dramatically. "You're a married man." She flipped her hair over her ear, playfully.

John smiled, "Yeah, yeah. I don't know how you get

anything done fighting off all our advances all day long."

"It's a real burden, but I get by," she sighed. "So, what's up?"

"I was curious about how you see me."

"How I see you?"

"The way I do things... Do you think I can be a little over the top when it comes to my approach with people? Am I too rash sometimes? Maybe a little too competitive?"

"Wow, Gail really got in your head today, didn't she?"

"No. It's not Gail. I'm just looking for some honest feedback."

"Feedback, huh?"

"Do I sometimes do things that tick you off?"

"I wouldn't say you tick me off. But you definitely have a competitive side—maybe a little too competitive for my taste. When you and Randy go head-to-head on some stupid contest—whoa!—get out of the way."

"That upsets you?" asked John.

"I don't know. It's just—we're a team, you know? And with you guys, it turns into this smack-talking, throw-down brawl. It kinda makes me uncomfortable— for me and, I'm sure, other people in the department. It's like, I start to wonder if I'm going to be the next one to get stepped on while the two of you punch and push your way to the finish line. You know what I mean?"

"Wow. I had no idea," said John. "But you realize

Randy and I have been going at it like that forever. We may talk a little trash, but there's no harm intended. We're buddies."

"Oh, I get that. I'm just saying. It seems like your 'friendly competition' sometimes comes at the expense of the team. You guys become, like, possessed. I find myself giving in to your ideas, just to get you two to back off a little. It's not because I necessarily agree with you."

John absorbed this. "I guess I could see how it might be tough for the rest of you."

"I don't know," said Leslie. "Maybe it's just those ridiculous sales contests. They bring out the Johnasaurus Rex."

John laughed. "Johnasaurus Rex?"

"Oh, had you not heard that before?"

* * *

Tyrannosaurus, meaning 'tyrant lizard,' was one of the largest land carnivores of all time. It was a fierce predator that walked on two powerful legs and...

"What'cha doing? Your kid's homework?"

John quickly closed out of the Web site window. In the doorway to his office, he found Randy—a wide grin filling his face. "Don't you ever knock?" asked John with a frown.

"Not when the door is open." Randy flopped his oversized frame into one of John's side chairs and motioned to John's computer. "What's with the dinosaurs?"

"Did you know about this Johnasaurus nickname?"

Randy laughed. "Of course."

John shook his head. He didn't quite know whether to take it as a compliment or an insult.

"It's better than mine," admitted Randy.

"Why, what's yours?"

"If you don't know, I ain't tellin.'"

"I guess I've been left out of the nickname loop."

"Is this what your voicemail was about?" asked Randy. "Your stupid nickname?"

"No."

"Well if you're looking for the secret behind my latest beat-down of team 'extinction,' I'm pretty sure you're..."

John's mind wandered as Randy droned on. Was there a word for overdone trash-talking? If so, Randy was pictured next to the definition. It was a skill Randy must have honed growing up on the asphalt basketball courts of his childhood and later as a college basketball star at some Big Ten school. You couldn't know Randy without knowing all about his glory days. His intense competitiveness made John second-guess asking him for feedback. But he also knew that he and Randy shared a lot of the same strengths. And after swallowing some jagged pills talking to Gail and Leslie, he figured he could use a little ego boost by talking to someone who played the game the same way he did.

Randy was still talking when John got up and shut the door. That got his attention.

"Whoa. That serious, huh?"

"No, biggie," said John, returning to his chair. "I just need to ask you something. And I want you to think before you respond—if that's even possible."

"Sure, brother. What's up?"

"I'm wondering if I ever do anything that creates conflict between us?"

Randy sat there and stared. Suddenly he burst out with laughter and stood up. "Man, that's rich," he said, moving toward the door.

"I'm serious."

"You been watching too much Oprah and Dr. Phil."

"So nothing causes conflict?" asked John.

"I thought we were cool? All in fun, right?"

"I know. I'm just making sure."

"Look, man. We're both fighters—hard-chargers. Varsity team. The rest of these fools got nothing on us. I actually like you pushin' me—makes me better. I've got no problem with that. Besides, I'm usually kickin' your butt every month."

"Yeah, that's what I figured," said John.

"The only thing I *don't* like is when you check out on me—don't shovel it right back. Takes the fun out of it."

"What are you talking about?"

"I don't know, man. Sometimes you kinda go vacant. The 'out-to-lunch' signs go up in your eyes."

"When does that happen?" asked John.

"Usually, you're unstoppable. Johnasaurus Rex,

right? But things go a little off-track, and you kinda run away, with your little dino tail between your legs."

"I don't do that."

"The hell you don't. Remember when I first started here? I was shadowing some of your calls with you. There was that one client. I forget his name. He sorta sucker-punched you with a contract issue—wanted to pull his business. You completely choked."

"I didn't choke," said John, defensively.

"Total deer in the headlights."

"I was thinking."

"You were stammering like a grade-schooler giving a book report. You coulda easily pulled through that situation. That part of the contract is always negotiable here. You choked, bro."

John's mind was racing after Randy left his office. John was trying to get feedback about his strengths, but this was something different—and he didn't like it. There was no appeal to being a 'fighter' who runs away during a fight. And yet that's how he was coming off to people? And to hear it from Randy made it all the more embarrassing. The fact was, John wasn't running away. He was thinking, strategizing. He had always been one to step back and assess the situation before attacking. Isn't that what all good generals do? Randy was all about shoot first, apologize later. How could that be better? John found himself anxious for his next rendezvous with Mac—whenever and wherever that turned out to be.

FIVE

JOHN CAREFULLY eased the door closed behind him and entered the darkened theater. He chuckled at the futility of his caution when he found the vast sea of red velvet seats empty. Aided by the faint aisle lighting, John made his way toward the darkened stage. The curtain was up, but the set was difficult to make out in the dim light. John began to wonder why Mac insisted on dark, obscure places for his meetings.

"Hello?" John called out.

Suddenly, the theater burst to life. A flood of red lights filled the stage, illuminating a painted backdrop, which resembled a European street scene—flower stand, bistro, old-world architecture. John stood and stared into the intense, dream-like glow emanating from the stage.

"Ladies and Gentlemen, Mister John Doyle!" Mac's voice boomed from the house speakers.

John looked around, trying to locate the source of

the voice.

"Up here," called Mac, no longer using the microphone.

John found him, waving from the side of the stage.

"Come on up."

John made his way to the stage, where he was overcome by the aroma of fresh paint and sawdust. The Italian bistro was really just a plywood facade suspended from a web of ropes and wires that trailed into the dark void beyond the burning red stage lights. He hadn't been on a stage since elementary school, and he could count on one hand the number of times he'd been an audience member—twice for his kids' school performances and a few plays Nancy had dragged him to. Now, he was center-stage, basked in red light before 300 empty seats.

"You look good up there, John. Ever done any acting?"

"Nah. I was kind of a jock in high school."

Mac carried two café chairs to the front edge of the stage and positioned them facing the set.

"You're not going to make me perform, are you?" asked John, apprehensively.

"Why? Is that out of your comfort zone?" asked Mac with a sly grin.

"Seriously?"

Mac laughed. "No, I'm not going to make you perform. Although my wife is always looking for new talent. She directs a couple shows here every year. And when she's not directing, she's acting or helping out with all of the others."

"That's impressive," said John.

"Well, it's glorified community theater. But she loves it. She studied acting in college and probably could have had a decent career, but I charmed her away from Broadway. Now, I'm forced to pay for that transgression by volunteering as the set-builder-in-residence."

"Ah. You and your trusty tools."

"Exactly."

"So what now? Will you be performing a play for me on conflict?"

"Not exactly, but I do want to play with some concepts a little today." Mac sat down in one of the café chairs. "But first, have a seat. I'm curious how your feedback homework went. What did you discover?"

John opened his notepad and took a seat in the other chair.

"Well, it was kind of all over the place."

"That would make sense," said Mac.

"How so?"

"You talked to multiple people, right?"

"Yeah?"

"It'll start to make sense very soon," said Mac, reassuringly. "Tell me what you learned."

"Well, people seem to think I overdo my strengths— some more than others. And different people mentioned different strengths. I know my boss thinks I'm far too loud in my *quickness to act* and *self-confidence*. She'd like the volume turned way down on those." John squinted at his notes. He wasn't used to the intense, red light. "And then with my buddy Randy—we're pretty similar in a lot of ways—he didn't have any complaints with the way I act, except when things get tough."

"That's interesting. Explain what you mean there."

"Randy is a pretty focused, go-getter type like I am. But I guess when conflict starts, he's instantly ready to pick up the bat and start swinging. I don't do that. I kinda step back and think about what's going on before I feel ready to dive into the fight. That's where Randy found frustration working with me. I mean, is that so wrong? Shouldn't we all think before we act?"

Mac looked at John and grinned. "This is going to be a good day. I can feel it." Mac jumped out of his chair, clearly bursting with anticipation.

"You didn't answer my question."

"I promise you," said Mac, "you won't leave this stage before you can answer those questions yourself. I'm going to walk you a little further through the theory of Relationship Awareness—try to help you better understand the nature of conflict. Good?"

"OK, Doc," sighed John.

Mac began pacing. "Since we're on a stage, let me ask you a question about acting."

"That wouldn't be my favorite *Jeopardy!* category, but I'll give it a try."

"Do you know what method acting is?"

"I've heard the term, but I'm not sure I could explain it," said John.

"Basically, method acting relates to techniques actors use to create in themselves the thoughts and emotions of the characters they're playing. They don't just act the emotion, they recreate the emotion in themselves by identifying what their characters must be feeling."

"Like putting yourself in someone else's shoes?" asked John.

"In a way, yes. You'll often hear a method actor ask the director, *'What's my motivation?'* They're trying to determine where the character is coming from. What they're after."

"Got it."

"Well," continued Mac, "just as a method actor needs to figure out the purpose driving his character's actions to create a convincing performance, we need to take the time to ask the same question."

"What's my motivation?" repeated John.

"Exactly. If we want to have productive relationships, we need to figure out what our motivation is and—perhaps more importantly—what the other person's motivation is."

"How does knowing that make our relationships more productive?" asked John.

"Remember what we talked about last time? Behavior can be deceiving. It's more important to know why someone is doing something, in order to understand their intent and avoid letting misinterpretations cause you conflict."

"Kind of like you were talking about with my over-done strengths," said John. "Gail may be seeing rash behavior in me, but she might be less inclined to go into conflict over it if she knew it was really just my desire to act quickly. All I'm trying to do is jump on an opportunity and get things accomplished."

"Right! And when she understands that," said Mac, "all of a sudden, the behavior she's been perceiving as rash can be seen in a different light. She can begin to see it as your true motivation of wanting to achieve results—which I hardly think she'd find issue with."

"And yet it seems like she always does," said John. "I can do something that I think is absolutely right, and it seems as if she sees it as absolutely wrong. I'm really surprised sometimes at how we see the same issue so differently—like we're not even living in the same world."

"That's where it becomes important to understand: *'What's her motivation?'*"

"Wouldn't she be motivated by results, too?" asked John.

"I'm sure results are of value to her, but the way you've described her, there may be other things that are even more important to her. What motivates you may not be what motivates others. The problem is that most people don't know this. They assume everyone views the world the way they do. And if they do know, it's sometimes hard to put that knowledge into practice. Our filter is pretty hard to get around."

"What do you mean by *filter*?"

Mac walked to the side of the stage and grabbed something. "You've heard the term *rose-colored glasses,* right?" asked Mac.

"Sure, like for someone who only sees things positively," answered John.

"People who view the world through rose-colored glasses have a 'filter' of optimism that affects the way they interpret what happens around them. That same concept is really true for all of us. Only instead of it being 'optimism,' it's our motivational values that filter our perceptions. We interpret what we see others do through our own set of standards."

Mac returned to his chair. In his hand, John saw what appeared to be some sort of oversized remote control.

"What do you see there?" asked Mac, pointing to the painted facade.

"It's a backdrop," said John.

"Yes, but describe it. What setting does it create? What is the mood?

"It looks like a city street in someplace European. Italy, I'd guess," offered John. He sensed a trick question and looked at the set carefully.

"Is it a nice place?" asked Mac.

"Looks pretty nice. It reminds me of a trip Nancy

and I took before the kids were born. Venice, then Florence. It was beautiful."

Mac just smiled at John. He pointed the remote and jabbed a button with his thumb. Instantly, the lights popped from red to green.

"Pretty tricky," said John.

"I'm also the lighting director," said Mac. "So now, what do you see?"

John looked back at the street scene. In the thick, green light, the same walls of the buildings were now marred with graffiti. The shop windows were splintered with cracks.

"Looks like a war zone," said John.

"Maybe this is what the same situation looks like to someone like Gail. With her green-colored filter, things look pretty different. Can you see how that could cause conflict? Like you described: same world, but very different view of it."

"Wow, so I'm just out there, living in la-la land while the rest of the world sees everything a different way?" asked John.

"I'm just using this setting as an illustration of filters. You mentioned Randy having pretty similar views to you. Would you say his motivation is also concerned with getting things done and achieving results?"

"Definitely."

Mac hit the button again, and the lights reverted back to red. The Italian bistro returned to its pristine state. "So his filter is pretty close to your own in most situations."

"That makes sense," said John. "But why do you say most situations? If our motivational values are the same, wouldn't we always see things the same?"

"When all is well, that's probably true. But when faced with conflict, suddenly, our motivation can change completely. And when that happens, your filter changes too."

John stood up. He was feeling energized, as so many pieces were falling into place. "That explains why Randy doesn't understand my approach to conflict. We usually share a filter, but conflict comes along and shakes things up."

"Exactly! You're both running along in Red Land, and then something happens to you that sends you off course."

Mac hit the switch to fill the stage in Green again.

"You're in conflict now," declared Mac. "A new filter has washed over you. Meanwhile, Randy is still seeing red and can't understand what happened to his red running buddy. You stop making sense to him."

"And this happens to everyone?" asked John, his mind racing.

Mac considered the question a moment. "Tell me about your wife."

"Huh?"

"What do you think Nancy's motivation is?"

"I don't know," said John warily.

"If anyone would, you would. Think about it."

John was taken aback by the question. He had been in such a work-life mindset that he had yet to let his home life be a factor. But it made perfect sense when he thought about it. His work with Dr. Mac was about conflict and his relationships. There was no distinction between work and home when he looked at it at that level.

Mac was still staring at him, waiting for an answer. John first thought about Nancy's behaviors. Perhaps they would offer clues into her motivation.

"I'd say she's pretty loving and caring. Always very supportive."

"OK, but you need to get to the *why*. Just like your ambition serves your desire to achieve and get things done, what desire does her supportiveness serve?"

"She truly wants to help people."

"OK, good."

Mac grabbed John by the arm and walked him to the upper right side of the stage. "Stand there," Mac directed, as he walked back to the chairs. He snatched them up and placed one at center-stage, close to the edge. Then he positioned the other one directly across from John on the upper left side of the stage. After making a few adjustments with the chairs' positioning, Mac walked to the center—between John and the two chairs.

"Ready for this?" asked Mac, almost giddy with anticipation.

"Trust, Doc," offered John, dryly. "I'm pulling that tool from the depths of my toolbox."

"Good man."

Mac flicked a button on his remote, and the light shifted quickly. John found himself again flooded in red light, but this time, the light came at him from behind, creating a swath of red along the stage. John's black shadow stretched to where Mac stood. John could also see that the chair at the edge of the stage was lit with a green spotlight. The other chair was in Blue. All three colors combined at the center creating an almost white light where Mac stood at the hub. The overall effect was a three-color triangle on the battered wood floor of the stage.

"Welcome to the seven motivational value systems," said Mac, proudly.

"Does that mean we left Italy?"

"We've taken a journey to the clusters of motives that are used by individuals in their quest for self-worth. When things are going well, these are the certain blends of values that work together to drive our behavior."

"OK, Doc. You lost me."

"Let's say this entire triangle of light on the floor represents the one, unifying thing every human being wants—the desire to feel worthwhile."

"Self-worth," recalled John.

"Right. It's the ultimate motivation we all share. We want to feel good about ourselves. Gail wants that.

Nancy wants that. Randy wants that. But *how* each of us obtains that for ourselves can be different—hence the multiple colors—Red, Green, and Blue. The things that generate feelings of self-worth in some people may not generate the same feelings of self-worth in others. But the goal is ultimately still the same."

"So my route to self-worth is Red?" asked John.

"Exactly. The Red approach is *Assertive-Directing,* with a concern for task accomplishment and the organization of people and resources to achieve results."

"That sounds about right."

"Absolutely. Plus, you took an assessment that told me you were," said Mac with a wink. He walked to the Blue area. "Now, if you're right about Nancy, she sits over here in the Blue chair. People in this *Altruistic-Nurturing* area of the triangle achieve self-worth when they can focus on the protection, growth, and welfare of others. They want to help people."

"Does that mean Gail sits over in the Green chair?" asked John.

Mac moved that way. "Probably. The Green part of the triangle is the *Analytic-Autonomizing* area. They have a concern for precision and establishing and maintaining order. Self-worth is achieved when they have assurance that things have been properly thought out."

"That would be Gail, all right," said John. "So where are the other four colors?"

"What do you mean?" asked Mac.

"You said there were seven motivational thingys."

"Motivational value systems. That's true. There are seven, but they're all just an interplay of these three, core motivations. The other four are blendings of them. When motives combine, they make new areas. Just like here in the center where Red, Green, and Blue combine to make the Hub of the triangle. This group is called *Flexible-Cohering.*" Mac walked to the center, where the light turned white. "This area is focused on the group— members of the group, welfare of the group, belonging in the group. Since it's a fairly equitable blend of Blue, Red, and Green, the people in this area can often relate easily to people of other regions of the triangle. I'm actually a Hub, myself. I find self-worth by being flexible and open-minded."

"Is that why you can't stand being in your office? You just want to mix it up a little?" asked John.

Mac laughed. "Maybe so." He held up his lighting remote. "But I also don't have this in my office."

"True. You definitely couldn't pull off your light show there." John walked halfway to the chair under the blue light and stopped. "So would this be a blended motivational value system?"

"Exactly. You're in the area of Red-Blue, a.k.a. the *Assertive-Nurturing* folks. People in that area share a little from the Red side and a little from the Blue side.

NOTE: for a color illustration of the triangle and all 7 Motivational Value Systems, check out the Character Assessment Results in the back of this book.

Self-worth is achieved with a concern for helping others, while using task accomplishment and leadership."

Mac took a spot between the Red and Green lights. "This is the *Judicious-Competing* group. They show a concern for rational leadership, strategy, and fairness in competition. A little Red with a little Green."

John crossed over to the Blue-Green blend, "So these guys want to help people analytically?"

"In a way, yes. That's the *Cautious-Supporting* area. They want to thoughtfully help people help themselves."

"Wow. That's a lot of different kinds of people to have to figure out," said John.

"Well, it's helpful to look at it as three primary drives working together to yield these seven basic personality types. But even within these seven, you'll find variation, just as you do here on the floor, when the colored lights mix in varying degrees. Even two people in the Red part of the triangle may have varying degrees of Red. Randy, for example, may be with you in the Red part of the triangle, but he may be closer to the tip or maybe near one of the blend areas, like Red-Green. You relate to him well because he's close by—not because he's identical to you."

"Are you saying that even if I'm Red, I also have some Green and Blue?" asked John.

"You're a mixture which is predominantly Red. Think of it like this: If we were making a bunch of different kinds of ice cream, the recipes for each flavor share most of the same ingredients. But a few things stand out in each one to make it the flavor we identify when we see and taste it. For the most part, every person has a little of everything. We just sometimes prefer one set of ingredients over others, which gives us our flavor. You gravitate more toward the Red values than the Green and Blue ones."

"So I have a Red flavor," said John.

"And I'm kind of a Neapolitan here in the Hub," said Mac.

John walked around the triangle slowly. With each step, he thought about the meaning of the shade of color his foot landed on.

"There's a decent amount of complexity in the human condition, isn't there?" Mac inquired.

"You're telling me. It would sure be a lot easier if everyone came from Red Land."

"True, but how dysfunctional would that be? Who's going to follow your leadership? Who's going to handle the details? You need the helpers and the thinkers and everyone else on this triangle. Quite frankly, all this diversity is good."

"But good isn't always easy," said John, meekly.

"It gets easier. That's why we're working together."

John nodded. He was still staring at the colored lights spread across the floor.

"So if we're all just trying to do the right thing, how do we end up dealing with so much conflict?" asked John.

"Well, as we all stand in our respective spots, trying

to do the right thing to maintain our own sense of self-worth, conflict can happen when our *right* thing appears to be the *wrong* thing to another person across the triangle."

"There's so much conflict because there are so many things that can set it off," said John

"Unfortunately, that's true. But let's break it down—make it a little more manageable."

"Gladly," said John.

"You said Gail found your approach in certain situations not to her liking. True?"

"Very true," admitted John.

Mac walked down and sat in the Green-lit chair. "Can you now start to see why that may be?"

"She's Green, and I'm Red?" said John.

"Well, that's a little oversimplified. Tell me what you think the dynamic is, considering the different motivational value systems at play."

"Well, she thinks I rush into things without thinking them through. She calls me impulsive. I think I'm just too hard-charging and competitive for her orderly, by-the-book sensibility. She wants to slow down and wait for data, while I want to speed up, so we don't miss an opportunity. She's so damn worried about policy that by the time she gets around to approving anything, we've missed the opportunity completely."

"It sounds as if she has some great strengths," Mac suggested.

"Great strengths? How do you figure?" John felt a pounding frustration well up inside of him. "It's impossible to get anything done around her. All she does is throw up roadblocks and slow down my progress. Sometimes I think she's intentionally trying to hold me and my team back with all of her nitpicking."

Just thinking about Gail got John worked up. He had become an expert at reciting these complaints. He'd happily offer an earful to anyone who would listen, and he was certain that Nancy was tired of hearing him vent about her—though she would never complain about it.

"I think you're starting to understand the nature of conflict, John." Mac offered gently.

"I am?"

"Jump out of your filter, and think about what you just said."

John looked at Mac, completely bathed in green light. He thought about how Mac defined the Analytic-Autonomizing values: logic, thoughtfulness, fairness... When he considered Gail's perspective, her *right thing* was to make sure everyone was moving in the correct direction taking into account all the facts. His own "irrational exuberance" probably scared her. It probably pushed her to operate way out of her comfort zone. Mac sat quietly, while John put the pieces together.

"We're causing each other conflict," said John. "Gail and I are both trying to do the right thing, based on our own reasons, but because these reasons—or, like you said, motivations—are filtering our perceptions, we feel conflict when we see behaviors that challenge our way of doing things. We're both trying to do our jobs the best way we know how, but our styles are so different that she thinks I'm working against her—and vice-versa."

Mac smiled. "That's what we call a breakthrough moment, John."

John felt a new sense of awareness and clarity wash over him. "Wow. And most of my top strengths are in direct opposition to her preferred way of doing things."

"And I would venture to guess that some of her top strengths are in direct opposition to your preferred way of doing things. What would you consider Gail's strengths to be?" asked Mac.

John chuckled. "I'm not sure that I'm the right person to answer that question."

"Oh, I think you are. You've already told me that Gail is orderly and cautious."

"Those are strengths?" John said, with more than a hint of sarcasm.

"Absolutely they are. So is being analytical. This world needs people who are organized, analytical, and cautious. Just like it needs people who are confident and ambitious. I may not like using my plumbing tools, but I sure am glad there are people who do. I rely on those people. I have them on my speed-dial."

"OK, I could see that."

"Maybe you're struggling to find Gail's strengths

because you're stuck seeing her as a frustration. Try this technique: think about what bugs you and then find the positive side. In other words, trace back her strengths from the overdone strengths."

John chuckled. "You know what? I already did this with her. When I was asking for feedback, I started to get annoyed by her incessant analysis paralysis, and I forced myself to look for the strength."

"That's fantastic, John. So this should be easy."

John took a deep breath and gave it a go. "Basically, Gail is very logical and methodical. She thinks things through, which helps us avoid making bad decisions. She also establishes guidelines and makes sure everything is clear and thorough. Oh, and whenever there's a sales contest or new bonus plan, she works really hard to make sure that it's a level playing field for everyone."

"And what is the strength at play there?" asked Mac with a look John couldn't decipher.

"I guess *fairness*? Which I totally respect... I don't want anyone coming back after I beat the socks off 'em and saying that I had some sort of advantage," said John.

"Fairness. Interesting. I seem to remember *fair* being one of your strengths."

"Yeah, I guess that's true. So what does that mean?"

"That's a great illustration of the distinction between behaviors and motivation. You may share a strength like fairness but use that tool for different reasons. Same behavior—different motivation," explained Mac. "Has

Gail's behavior of *fair* ever caused you conflict?"

"Not that I can think of."

"Why would it?" said Mac. "But it's clear to see how someone who's quick to act might upset someone who's cautious and methodical. Or how someone who is reserved might react to someone who's brimming with self-confidence."

"Absolutely," said John.

"And that's just a contrast of plain old strengths— not even their overdone counterparts."

"So then what can I do about it?" asked John.

"About what?"

"What do I do to keep from feeling conflict about her way of doing things?"

"You've already done it."

"I have? What have I done?"

"You've started to understand where she's coming from," stated Mac, standing over the Green chair. "You can begin to see her behavior as merely a difference of style—not a direct challenge or threat aimed at annoying you or derailing you."

"That's it?" asked John.

"It's a good start. Oftentimes conflict is a choice, just like behavior is a choice. If you choose to continue to feel conflict over the way she does things, that's on you. Because now, you know she's just trying to do what she feels is right—using a behavior that brings her a feeling of self-worth."

John smiled to himself. He had to admit that even after one meeting with Mac, he had noticed a difference in his interaction with Gail. And after this afternoon, he was seeing her in a completely new light—a Green one to be exact. He knew Mac was right. Reaching an awareness of Gail's motivation gave John an undeniable feeling of understanding and respect for her. It made him almost anxious for the next opportunity to talk with her and see how this newfound appreciation would impact their relationship.

"Of course, conflict can come from other places, too," said Mac. "It's more than just a reaction to styles, behaviors, and overdone strengths. And in some cases, what people perceive as conflict is really something else. When people simply have different ideas about how to handle an issue, I call these disagreements *opposition*, rather than conflict. Opposition is often part of a healthy debate that leads us to better ideas."

"Yeah," agreed John, "I've found that brainstorming with people who have different points of view can be helpful in finding the best way to move forward on something."

"And that's productive," said Mac. "In my mind, it can't be called conflict until it gets personal."

"Totally. With some people—in some situations—it starts to feel real personal. The difference is obvious."

"And that's an important distinction. I like to characterize conflict as the feeling that occurs when another person or set of circumstances becomes an obstacle that inhibits one's ability to live out their motivational values."

"Whoa, hold up there, Doc. Can you explain that?" John reached for his notepad.

"Sorry. That was maybe too Green a definition." Mac stood and moved to the Blue area. "People feel conflict when they can't be in their desired color space."

Mac grabbed the chair and brought it back to the edge of the stage next to the other one.

Mac continued. "When you were talking about Gail working against you at work, you looked pretty worked up."

"I felt pretty worked up," John confirmed.

Mac sat back down and hit a button on the lighting remote. The lights burst back to a red glow. John sat down next to Mac, ready for the next light show.

"So in those situations," said Mac, "you had an overwhelming emotional response—a feeling—brought on by Gail becoming an obstacle to your desire for achievement and getting things done."

"Right."

"She's blocking you from your desire to live in the Red—your 'happy place.' That's the feeling of conflict. Your sense of self-worth is threatened, and when that happens, your motivation changes in a predictable pattern. You feel pulled away from your happy place, which causes you to experience sequential changes in your motivation, which drive changes in your behavior."

"Huh? What do you mean *predictable pattern?*" asked John.

"Every person has a predictable and sequential pattern for how they experience changes in their motivation in the face of ongoing conflict. Essentially, conflict is experienced as a sequence of three, progressively serious stages and is often—but not always—evident to others, due to a change in behavior as well."

"I'm not sure I'm following."

"Well, let's revisit Randy's feedback. He noticed a real change in you in the face of conflict."

"That's what he said, yeah."

"Tell me what that change feels like to you," Mac said. "When Gail starts getting in your way, what do you do? When there's an issue at home, how does it feel?"

"Well, let's see. I guess my most common response is that I pull away and want to think about it. I go into my own analysis mode, trying to figure out what happened—who did what—and how I can work around it. I just want things to make sense."

The lights cut out with a bang. Darkness enveloped them, until a sharp circle of green light slowly appeared on the floor at the left side of the stage.

"That's your stage one," said Mac quietly. John could just make out his face in the darkness. "Now what if things persist? What do you do then?"

"I guess I get kind of angry if things don't get resolved. At that point, I come out swinging. And I'm pretty unbeatable, because I've had a lot of time to prepare my case. I've been known to fire my share of verbal missiles, and that almost always gets me in trouble. But at that point, I don't care."

Mac pressed more buttons on his remote and, boom!—a spotlight made a sharp, red circle of light on the floor at center-stage. "So that's your stage two," said Mac. "Then what?"

"I don't think there is a 'then what?'"

"So you've won every stage two battle? You've resolved every conflict?"

"No," admitted John, after some reflection.

"Stage three conflict can be tough. Many people only experience it a handful of times in their life. And it's never pretty or pleasant," said Mac.

"Well, when it's gotten to that stage, I guess I'm feeling pretty defeated. I've left it all on the field, and I've lost the will to fight."

Blue lights dropped on the right side of the stage. John looked at the three pools of light breaking the darkness of the theater.

"This is your Conflict Sequence, John."

The sight gave John a chill, for some reason. Maybe it was the darkness—or perhaps the subject matter. John shook it off and stood. He approached the small spotlight of green—his first-stage of conflict.

"I suppose we're all different in conflict too?" asked

John.

"There are thirteen possible Conflict Sequences."

"Different combinations of Red, Green, and Blue?" asked John.

"You got it," said Mac. "When most people think of conflict, they think of people angrily pointing their fingers and yelling at each other, don't they?"

"But that's just a Red response, right?" asked John. "Mine is more subtle. My wife says I sulk."

"But you're really just being cautious and assessing the situation. That's the Green response."

"And Blue?"

"A first-stage Blue response to conflict is about keeping the peace—giving in to try to smooth things over with the other person," Mac stated. "These are all common responses, but they're just behaviors—driven by a change in motivation. And that change is caused by your self-worth being threatened."

"They're pulling me away from my happy place—where I feel good about myself," concluded John.

"Exactly. And you run the risk of doing the same to other people—pulling them from their motivational value system. You deploy your strengths in support of your Red motivational values. Another person with different motivational values may see that behavior related to a particular issue as threatening to their self-worth, and it creates conflict in them."

"And then *they* experience a shift in motivation."

"Precisely. People only go into conflict about things that are important to them, so—if you think about it—that's a great opportunity."

"How so?"

"It's a learning opportunity. If we can recognize the source of the conflict—in other words, the trigger that launched the conflict—then we can learn what other people value and work to restore the sense of self-worth for the people involved."

"Actually help them out of their feelings of conflict?"

"Sure," said Mac. "When conflict is under control, all kinds of great things are possible."

Mac joined John at the pool of green light.

"Stage one is the most civilized. Here you're still able to focus on the whole picture. The issue, the other person... in stage one, you're still mindful of the factors outside yourself."

Mac moved away, stepping directly under the red spotlight, his features shadowed in the harsh light.

"As a conflict becomes deeper and more serious," said Mac, "a person in conflict becomes more narrowly focused on protecting self-worth and less focused on maintaining the relationship or solving the problem. The deeper the fall into our stages of conflict, the more damage is possible."

"Shouldn't we try to stay out of conflict altogether?"

"Ideally, yes," said Mac. "But that's not going to happen. There always seems to be someone or something out there, waiting to challenge our self-worth. What we can do is prevent the conflicts that are preventable and manage the conflicts that are inevitable. The ultimate goal is to minimize the visits to your deeper stages of conflict. Conflict can actually enhance your relationships. But that's more likely in stage one. When it hits stage two or three, you've lost concern for the relationship. Those verbal missiles you described can leave lasting scars."

"Scars they rarely let me forget," said John, sadly. "So as we're trying to manage a conflict situation, we need to figure out the other person's first-stage?"

"Actually, it's about learning to recognize the changes in behavior. Knowing what stage you're witnessing is a little harder. Two people in conflict might have different conflict sequences, *and* they don't necessarily cycle through their sequences at the same time. In fact, person 'A' might be deep in conflict because of the way they interpreted something that person 'B' did. Meanwhile, person 'B' isn't in conflict at all and doesn't even realize anything is wrong."

John laughed, "You might as well call person 'A,' *Nancy*, and person 'B,' *John*."

"Do you find it hard to know if she's in conflict?"

"Oh, it's not hard. It's painfully obvious. It just seems to come out of nowhere. Everything seems fine, and then I find out she's misinterpreted something I said days ago, and I don't have a clue until it's too late. She won't even let me explain. Does that mean she's first-stage Red?"

"Maybe not. You may be seeing second or third-stage Red."

"Really?"

"Well, by the time you hear about it, her focus has narrowed. She doesn't even want to hear your side. She's focused on herself at that point. What's more likely is she's first-stage Blue. You don't see it, because it's so similar to where she sits on the triangle."

"Which is also Blue," said John.

"The shift is there, but it's harder to see."

"So all those times she kept the peace and tried to smooth everything over, she was really in first-stage conflict?" asked John. But he already knew the answer. He started to realize that all these years, she wasn't avoiding conflict; her giving-in *was* her conflict—first stage conflict. When Mt. Saint Nancy erupted, she was already well into her conflict sequence. That couldn't be good.

A door opened backstage. Voices followed. Mac brought the plain white stage lights on with his controller and stood up.

"It's getting late. I think we've covered enough ground for one day."

John stretched, checking his watch, "Yeah, if I'm not on time tonight, I may be getting a healthy serving of second-stage Red for dinner."

"Let's pick this up later in the week. We'll be in touch."

"Homework?" asked John.

"Nothing specific. Just play with what you've learned. See what you notice. I wouldn't be surprised if the world looks a lot different to you now."

"Yeah," said John, "in shades of Red, Green, and Blue."

"And not necessarily in that order," Mac reminded him, with a smile.

SIX

A SURGE OF ANXIETY hit John as he scanned his calendar for the day. It was wall-to-wall appointments, and the message light was already blinking on his desk phone. He had only eight minutes before the sales meeting was to start, but with a day like today, every second was valuable. He pressed the message button on his phone and was about to enter his PIN when there was a knock on his open door. John looked up and saw Blake, one of his junior salesmen.

"I'm coming," said John, assuming he was collecting him for the meeting. "I was just going to check—"

"I think I need your help, John," interrupted Blake.

John reluctantly returned the phone to the cradle.

"Sure, Blake. What's up?" asked John with a hint of a sigh.

Blake took a seat on the edge of a chair. John noticed the dread in his eyes.

"It's Delta Systems."

"Oh, no. What?" asked John.

"Bonnie Sanstone wants to have a teleconference with us today at one. I think she's after another price concession and maybe some other breaks."

"You gotta be kidding."

"She's threatening to move all of her business. Everything."

John was instantly aware of the feeling of alarm that washed over him, pulling him into a deeper, darker, *Greener* place within his brain. He and Bonnie had locked horns many times over the years. She was Delta's purchasing agent and an infamously ruthless negotiator. The mere mention of her name sent John into a conflict reflex, like one of Pavlov's salivating dogs. He immediately started calculating the financial damage that would result if Bonnie followed through on her threat. Delta was not only Blake's biggest customer but also one of the biggest customers in the region. If Delta's orders dropped substantially, it would cause John to drop in every sales ranking that mattered. He would have almost no chance at winning any sales awards this year, and it certainly wouldn't help his chances for a promotion.

"I know how you two have gone at it in the past," said Blake, "but I don't think I can do this alone. She's my biggest customer—by far."

"Oh, I hear ya."

"If we don't give her what she wants..." Blake trailed

off, as if finishing his thought would somehow make it a reality.

"She's already got us down to next to nothing," said John.

"I know, but I don't know what else to do. If I lose this account, I mean... I'm screwed for the entire year. I won't make my numbers, and my commission check won't buy me lunch."

John shifted uncomfortably in his chair.

Blake continued his plea, "And Maria is still at home with the baby... Those commission checks are all that's keeping us going."

John was already deep in thought about how to keep Delta's business. He knew that it was going to be a battle. Bonnie was well aware that she was one of Starr's biggest accounts and she happily played that card at every opportunity.

John glanced at the clock. The eight minutes had raced by, and now, he and Blake were going to be late for Gail's staff meeting.

"We gotta go," said John, as he stood up.

"Can you help me out on this?" asked Blake.

"Of course. No problem. We'll get this worked out," said John, confidently. But deep inside, John's thoughts were spinning like a top.

* * *

Gail's opening monologue was well under way as John

and Blake found seats at the far end of the narrow conference room. John purposely avoided making eye contact with Gail. He noticed Randy across the room, a smug grin filling his face. Randy discreetly tapped his oversized, overpriced watch. It was his first salvo of the day. John remained unfazed though; his mind was busy with the impending teleconference with Bonnie. His brain tore through all of the possible scenarios at lightning speed. John smiled to himself at the recognition that he was fully engulfed in his first-stage Green conflict.

Since the agenda was fairly light, Gail adjourned the meeting in 40 minutes, and John was quickly on his feet and making his way toward the door. With only one step to freedom, John felt Randy's big hand on his shoulder.

"Hold up there, Johnny D," said Randy. "You, sir, were tardy."

"What are you, the hall monitor?"

"If that means I can bust your chops, then yes."

"I gotta run," said John moving into the hall.

Randy followed, "What's wrong with you, man? You alright?"

John turned to him. He thought about the feedback Randy had given him, and he realized this was a perfect example of Randy feeling a disconnect because of John's shift to Green conflict. He wanted to keep walking but figured this would be an opportunity to make a different choice.

"Sorry, man," said John. "I'm just a little distracted.

Delta Systems is looking to grind us down again."

"Is that Bonnie? She's tough, bro."

"You have no idea. She's prepared to jump ship if I don't give in to her demands."

Randy scowled, "You gotta stand up to that woman. She's been playin' that game with our company for years. Time to shut that down, you know? She needs us just as much as we need her."

"Easy for you to say. If she takes her business across town, I'm hosed. Blake's hosed. The whole company would feel that one."

"I'm just tellin' you what I'd do. Don't give in, buddy," said Randy, as he held out a fist. "Be strong."

John met Randy's knuckles with his own, but as he watched Randy walk away, he knew this call wasn't going to be as simple as flexing a little muscle. Too much was at stake.

* * *

The morning had raced by, and John felt impending doom churning in his gut as the clock on his desk hit 12:55. Dr. Mac hadn't returned his call yet. There would be no advice—no pep talk. He was on his own for this one.

John had spent some time over lunch trying to think back on his interactions with Bonnie over the years. What could her motivation be? From everything he remembered, it was looking like Green or Red. There were signs that could point to either one. She always came to a conversation fortified with an arsenal of data, which she quoted with whiz-kid dexterity. But unlike Gail's exacting and reserved delivery (or Green-speak as John was starting to call it), Bonnie spoke with a passionate, no-nonsense, results-driven approach that reminded him of his own. After an exhausting internal debate, he remembered the blends. He didn't have to choose one; she was probably both—a Red-Green blend. She wanted to win, but only if she had an indisputable, rational case for it. John hoped he was right about her, since the last hour had been spent planning a Red-Green strategy for the conference call.

12:59. Ready or not, John dialed the designated number and punched in the passcode. An automatic greeting welcomed him to Delta's teleconference center. Blake was already on the line.

"Hello?" said John.

"It's just us, boss." said Blake. "I hope you have a plan."

"Actually, I think I do."

A few seconds later, a chime announced Bonnie's arrival on the call.

"Good afternoon, everyone," said Bonnie.

"Hello, Bonnie," offered John.

"How are you, Bonn?" asked Blake.

"Fine, thanks."

"How'd your husband's trip to Thailand go?" asked Blake. John cringed. Blake's love for chit-chat had always struck him as superfluous and inane. Since working with Mac, though, John realized Blake's best weapon in sales had been his ability to build close relationships with his clients. This, however, was not the time or the person for it. John imagined that Bonnie had prepared for this call even more than they had. She had her chess board lined up, and she was itching to start moving the pieces.

"It was fine," said Bonnie, flatly.

"So..." John jumped in to block any more Blue chatter from Blake, "I hear we have some things to talk about."

"You know, I've done business with you guys a long time," said Bonnie. "And I'd like to stick with you, but I've got orders to cut costs. And quite frankly, one of your competitors has offered prices that are significantly better than yours. So as much as it would pain me to do it, I'm afraid I need to make a switch."

John's stomach dropped. "Did you sign a contract with them?"

"Well, not yet. But we're talking some big numbers. We're going to need a much deeper discount."

There it was. Even though John knew this was coming all day, it still packed a punch.

"It's just business. You understand," said Bonnie, casually.

"I understand," said John. It wasn't the sarcastic response he wanted to give, but he was doing his best to stay composed. He knew being baited into conflict would take the conversation down a destructive path—

one he would not have as much control over. He took a deep breath and pulled on his 'Red-Green hat.'

"We've obviously been here before, Bonnie, and I know you have a job to do," said John. "You're responsible for managing your company's resources and making sure your production people have what they need to get the job done, right?"

"Look, I just need some better numbers, John. That's it."

"I know, and I respect that. What I hope to do during our conversation today is to understand and address what's really important to you. I've got some facts I'd like to share, and ultimately, I think I can offer a winning strategy that makes sense for both of us. I really think we can work together on this."

"OK," Bonnie said, with a hint of caution.

"I'm confident we can find an equitable way forward that works well for everyone concerned."

John read that line word-for-word from his notes. It was the most Red-Green statement he could think of for the situation. He held his breath and waited for her reaction.

"That would be perfect. Let's hear some of those facts..." said Bonnie.

John wanted to jump up and down. He wondered if his smile could be heard on the other end of the call.

For the duration of the 45-minute conversation, John did his best to stay in a Red-Green mindset. He listened and acknowledged Bonnie's position. He confidently presented Starr Industries' record of superior service, product performance data, and offered a comprehensive market analysis, showing Starr's price points in comparison with the market overall. Throughout the conversation, Bonnie remained engaged and even softened her line-in-the-sand approach. In the end, they agreed to continue the relationship with a slight reduction in the price of four items. He also got her to agree to a two-year contract extension, instead of the usual one. In the end, the call could be considered a big win for John and for Starr Industries.

Within seconds of the teleconference ending, John's phone rang. He smiled as he recognized Blake's number.

"Are you OK with that outcome?" asked John.

"OK? I'm thrilled," exclaimed Blake. "I've never seen anyone handle Bonnie like that. You had her eating out of your hand. How'd you pull that off?"

"I just tried a different approach this time. Instead of letting her put me on the defensive, I tried to understand how she thinks and where she's coming from. The thing with Bonnie is, you just have to make your case. And make it bulletproof."

"You're a magician."

"I don't know about that, but I do think we're in a pretty good place with Bonnie and her book of business."

"I'm grateful, boss. You'll have to teach me how you did that."

"You just gotta have a nice conflict," said John smiling to himself.

"Have a what?" asked Blake.

"Never mind," said John, with a chuckle.

* * *

John was still high off his win with Bonnie as his house came into view. Nancy had sat through many stories over the years about the drubbings John had taken from the "evil purchasing agent from Delta." He was excited to finally share some good news. His time with Mac was really starting to pay off.

And then John made the mistake of going inside.

The instant he entered the house, he could tell all was not well in the Doyle household. The shrill sobs from Emma shook the walls—not panicked shrieks of pain but the weary, unrelenting wail of a toddler in need of a pillow and pacifier. J.J. could also be heard shouting something about school.

John thought seriously about ducking back into the garage, but Nancy came around the corner wielding a vacuum cleaner. She met him with a sour look.

"You don't answer your texts anymore?" snapped Nancy.

"What's going on?" asked John, not really wanting to know the answer.

"You have no idea what today's been like, John."

She kept walking, leaving him speechless in the

doorway. It was clear to John that his response in this moment would determine the course of the entire evening. But the more he thought about the right thing to say, the more his thoughts dissolved into incoherence.

"Seriously?" Nancy was back, staring at him in astonishment. "You just going to stand in the doorway all night?"

"It's been a long day, Nance," said John as he moved past her. All he wanted was the opportunity to drop his briefcase off in his home office—maybe steal a minute or two to regroup.

"Don't even think about it," hissed Nancy.

"What?"

"What do you think? Whenever there's a crisis around this house, you run and hide in your office."

"I'm going to put my stuff down. Is that alright with you?" said John with a punch of sarcasm.

"Whatever. See you in an hour."

"I'm not *hiding*!" John responded sharply. "I just know how emotional you get over every little thing."

John was already on his way down the hall when he heard the vacuum hit the floor. The sound and what it meant made him wince. Instantly, she was on his heels.

"Little things? You mean like our children?"

"Look, Nancy—"

"Your son is refusing to ever go back to school!"

"Can you just calm down, so we can talk about this?"

"How about this for calm," said Nancy, "I'm going

to go to the gym for the first time this week, and *you* can feed the kids their dinner, *you* can make sure the homework gets done, and *you* can get them ready for bed. *Then* we'll talk about calm."

As Nancy wheeled around and marched away, John's thrill of victory at work was replaced by the agony of defeat in his own home. How could he have dealt with one conflict so expertly and fallen so flat on his face with the next? Tonight's conflict had happened with an enormous absence of *nice*. Clearly, he needed more help. His next appointment with Dr. Mac was only hours away. Still, it was too far to avoid sleeping on the sofa that night.

SEVEN

THE AFTERNOON SUN glistened in a brilliant blue sky. The gently swaying ocean stretched to eternity beyond the weathered rails of the long pier. But inside John's throbbing head, the grey clouds churned. Not even this postcard setting could cut his sour mood. The previous night's fight with Nancy had gone unresolved, and John was wallowing in frustration. Just when he thought he was getting a hold of this conflict stuff, he got the wind knocked out of him at home.

Halfway down the pier, John began to question whether he was supposed to meet Mac at the end of the pier or the start. All he could see up ahead of him were a handful of hardcore fishermen. A gentle breeze carried with it the rancid smell of dead fish. John immediately regretted being in a suit and tie and began removing his coat.

"John!"

John turned back and saw Mac skewering a pink and white squid on his fishing line. John had walked right past him, as he was decked out in ratty shorts and a floppy hat.

"Oh, hey, Doc," said John, flatly.

"I see you dressed for the occasion," said Mac, looking over John's out-of-place silk tie and black slacks.

"I had a client meeting. I didn't realize we were going to be deep-sea fishing today."

"I love it out here. Great place for conversations."

"And here I thought you only liked meeting in dark places," said John, recognizing the contrast between here and his last two meeting spots.

"Not on a gorgeous day like today. Beautiful, isn't it?"

John shrugged, laid his suit coat over the back of the bench next to Mac, and loosened his tie.

Mac studied John, and asked "Everything OK?"

"Rough night," said John, reluctantly. "Great day, but didn't end so great."

"You want to talk about it?"

John looked over the rail at the waves crashing below. "Any bites?"

"Not yet," said Mac, letting John's avoidance slide. "But some of the guys were saying the striped bass were biting. Are you a fisherman?"

"Not really," said John, removing his tie.

"I've got an extra rod here for you, if you'd like to give

it a try."

Mac readied his stance and prepared to cast his line. John followed the graceful arc of the bait until it splashed in the water, 15 yards out.

"That's the spot!" said Mac triumphantly.

Mac made it look easy. John turned up the sleeves on his starched shirt and picked up the spare rod and reel. He figured he could use the distraction. In his younger days, John would go running or meet the guys for a game of basketball to blow off a little steam. But it had been years since he'd done that. Maybe he should try to work some exercise back into his life. It certainly couldn't hurt.

"Go ahead, John. Give it a try," said Mac.

The heavy rig felt good in his hands. It had been a lifetime since John had been fishing. He'd never particularly cared for the "sport"—too much waiting around. What he did love was the memories it brought back—camping with his dad, enjoying the outdoors up in Bridgeport every summer. Maybe he and J.J. should plan a trip up North with his dad, three generations of Doyles, floating around in his dad's aluminum boat, hunting rainbow trout. John hoped he wouldn't forget to plan something.

The rod was already rigged with a large hook and heavy weights for the ocean. John reached into the small cooler full of squid and gingerly picked one up by a tentacle.

"Just push one of those onto your hook," instructed Mac.

"Got it."

By this point, John had given up trying to salvage his clothes and wiped his wet hands on his slacks. With bait and hook ready, John visualized the "perfect spot" for the cast—just a little farther out than where Mac's line emerged from the water. Then with everything he had, John whipped the pole overhead and released the line. The soft clicking noise stopped abruptly as the reel seized and the tackle jerked back toward him and smacked somewhere underneath the pier. Instantly, John felt his face grow hot. A few gentle tugs on the rod failed to free the line. He cranked the reel to try a little more pressure on the line and flicked the rod a few times straight up, then to the right, then to the left. Still, the line remained fastened somewhere beneath the pier.

John's frustration set in quickly. He had done everything perfectly. Something must have been wrong with the reel. A few more quick flicks of the pole rendered no results. He stole a glance at Mac, who had to have noticed John's struggle, but Mac's eyes were fixed on the horizon. That's OK, he thought. He didn't really want help anyway. He was confident he could figure this out on his own. John set the rod aside and leaned over the rail, looking for some clue as to where the hook had gotten hung up. When that proved futile, he searched for a possible route down. John quickly ruled that option out, as he suddenly felt the heights get to him. There was simply nothing he could think of to free his line.

John snatched the rod back and started yanking the pole upwards. With each increasingly strong snap, the pole contorted into impossible forms. The damn thing just wasn't going to budge. John knew the battle was lost. Deflated, he dropped the pole against the pier railing and stepped away. So much for a relaxing afternoon of fishing! He was feeling more gloomy than ever.

"Here." Mac handed him a pocketknife.

It was 'game over.' John resigned himself to the failure, leaned as far over the railing as he dared, and sacrificed the hook with a slice of the blade.

"So what happened there, John?"

"I cast my line, but something got hung up—"

"No, John," interrupted Mac. "I don't care about the fish story. What happened with you?" He tapped John on the chest. "In here."

"I just experienced conflict with a pink squid."

"OK, tell me about it."

John expelled a frustrated laugh.

"Every experience is a learning experience, no?" said Mac.

John was in no mood to play along. Mac set his rod down and crossed his arms.

"Tell me, John," said Mac. "How long are you going to let conflict control you? How much longer are you willing to let situations like this ruin your day. Look at it out here. It doesn't get any nicer. And you're moping around like a rain cloud is following you."

"You're right," John acknowledged. Mac's words helped expose a weariness within him. He really was tired of the dark cloud. "I'm sorry."

"No reason to be sorry. I get it. I just don't want you to stay in that place and waste this time we have together."

"Neither do I."

"OK, so tell me about your little fishing adventure. I witnessed something there that I hope you saw too."

"I saw me make a fool of myself," said John.

"When you were casting your line, what was going on in your head?"

John considered the question. In an instant he recognized his Red motivational value system calling the shots—the surge of competitiveness as he watched Mac cast his line flawlessly, the ambition of choosing a spot farther out, how quickly the whole incident had happened. He had barely secured the bait before he was hurling it out into the water.

"I saw my goal, I set the bar ridiculously high, and my mind was 10 steps ahead of my body," said John.

"That's interesting. What were you thinking about?"

"Not the fishing pole, that's for sure. I was thinking about my son... my dad. I hadn't even gotten my hook in the water, and I was already planning a fishing trip for all of us next summer. I was thinking about how much the equipment must cost..."

"You were everywhere but here," Mac observed.

"I guess I do that a lot. My head is in the future while I'm working in the present. I'm always thinking about the next great accomplishment—the next promotion—and as a result, I rarely enjoy what's happening right now. The present is never good enough."

"And how is that working for you?"

"You just saw it. I push too hard and think too little. Or at least think too little about what I'm doing at the moment. I just put too much force into it, and it came hurtling right back at me."

"Not the first time, I'm guessing."

"Story of my life," said John.

Mac picked up John's fishing pole and began to tie on a new hook.

John leaned against the rail. "Amazing how we can learn so much about ourselves by screwing up."

"Screwing up but also talking about what went wrong and why. That's the key. And you haven't even talked about the good stuff yet."

"What do you mean?" asked John.

"We figured out how your Red style got you into that predicament, but then, I got to witness the entire John Doyle conflict sequence in vivid color."

John had to think about that one. He remembered the three pools of light on the stage—Green, then Red, then Blue—representing his unique experience in conflict. It all started to fall into place for him.

"So conflict doesn't just have to be between people,"

said John—part question, part statement.

"All it takes is for your self-worth to be threatened," said Mac. "Did you feel that happening?"

"My self-worth? I guess I did. But not because I botched the cast. Because I was thinking about J.J.," admitted John. "It was like I was failing in front of him. And maybe the competitive side of me was embarrassed to screw up in front of you."

"And you accepted that invitation into conflict."

"What invitation?"

"You had a choice, right?" asked Mac.

"I suppose."

"Conflict feelings came calling, and you chose to let them in. You allowed those conflict feelings to progress."

"Which put me into my Green first-stage of conflict," said John. "I got really quiet and cautious—trying to figure out what to do. I was basically trying to analyze my way out of it."

"For a second there, I thought you were going to climb down and wrestle it out by hand." Mac laughed and shook his head.

"I was tempted." John was laughing, too. It occurred to John that his black cloud had dissipated. He felt the warm sun on his back like the arm of a friend.

"All for a 50-cent hook," said Mac with a wink. "So as soon as you transitioned out of your cautious, analysis mode, what happened?"

"I traded brain for brawn. I figured it was time to

muscle the thing loose. I was frustrated and started to get more aggressive."

"Stage two Red. Did that feel more productive or less productive?" asked Mac.

"It felt... I don't know—strangely satisfying at the time, but kind of out-of-control. I was letting my temper get to me."

"A few more wild tugs, and you may have found out just how much that equipment costs," scolded Mac playfully.

"Yeah," said John. "Like I said, 'out of control.'"

"Remember, in stage two conflict, your focus narrows to yourself and the problem. The well-being of my fishing pole was way out of your field of vision."

"I guess operating like that can be costly."

"Very much so. Costly to your relationships too."

Mac let that hang there. John took a seat on the bench as his thoughts immediately jumped to his ex-salesman Andy Ward, who had given John a scalding review in his exit interview. A few months before he left, Andy had forgotten to pass through a subcontractor price increase to a customer. It had risen into a big issue between all parties involved. John organized an emergency conference call with Andy and his customer and proceeded to hammer Andy on the facts. John was compelled to prove beyond a shadow of a doubt that Andy was at fault. In the end, the customer agreed to accept the pass-through cost, but that was probably the day Andy started updating his resume.

"It's kind of sickening, actually," said John "When I think about it, I've always been a staunch advocate for my team—would do whatever it takes to get them what they need to succeed. But when my feet are put to the fire, it's all about number one."

"Sounds unproductive," offered Mac.

The words from Andy's exit interview put a searing brand on his consciousness, *John Doyle was the main reason I started looking for another job.* John wondered how many conflicts he had "won" in stage two at the expense of the relationship. And if he was really so interested in the future, why was he was taking short-term victories that led to long-term losses? Was he grabbing short-term victories at home, too? He could not bear the thought of a long-term loss at home.

"I gotta stop going there," said John sincerely.

"Now there's a worthy goal for you," Mac affirmed. "Don't let yourself slide into stage two conflict."

Mac finished attaching the weights to the line and rested the rod against the railing. He took a seat next to John.

"Why do you think you let yourself go to stage two today?" asked Mac.

"There was no way that stupid hook was going to beat me. Not today."

"And yet..."

"It beat me," said John.

"Nooo!" kidded Mac. "You let a squid and a 50-cent hook take you all the way to stage three conflict? That dark, dreaded place?"

"If you want the 50 cents, I have it in my car."

"Don't worry about it," said Mac. "It was worth every penny. In less than 90 seconds, you got to live out your entire conflict sequence."

John thought about that final surrender he had just experienced. Stage three wasn't a place he had gone often—maybe three or four times. They were very unpleasant situations that he hoped to avoid ever seeing again. In fact, that place of defeat was why he argued so hard after his logic had failed him. In many ways, it wasn't about being right. It was about making sure he didn't get pushed to that last resort, where he would totally surrender.

"Stage three is an ugly place to be," said John.

"But it will always be lurking there—waiting for you to visit, should you choose to. That's what I meant by a predictable pattern. The emotional roller coaster you went through with this rod and reel is what you're likely to go through with conflict unless you resolve it or let it go."

"If I *choose* to," said John with extra emphasis.

"Exactly!" said Mac. "You, my friend, are well on your way to having a nice conflict."

"Boy, I hope so."

Mac held out a second small ice chest filled with

drinks. John removed a soda with a nod of thanks.

"There are really five keys to having a nice conflict," said Mac, as he popped the top off an iced tea. "Everything we've talked about thus far has given you the basic tools to excel in these areas; you need to *anticipate* conflict, know ways to *prevent* conflict, be able to *identify* conflict, know how to *manage* conflict, and find ways to *resolve* conflict. As you build skill in each of these areas, you'll find yourself enjoying productive, rewarding relationships with nearly everyone in your life."

John grabbed his notepad to quickly jot down the list.

"And don't worry," said Mac. "We'll take a closer look at each one. But first, I'm curious how your meeting went with your client. I'm sorry I wasn't able to get back to you in time."

"That's OK. Actually, it was... downright perfect."

"See, you're an expert already."

"Well, I thought so. Until I got home."

"Oh," said Mac. "Well, tell me about the meeting. I always like the good news first."

"Like I said in my message, one of my biggest clients was threatening to take her business elsewhere. Her name's Bonnie—a real nightmare—usually makes me crazy. But all through the morning, leading up to the conference call, I recounted all my past interactions with her and realized she was probably a blend of Red and Green. I thought about her role and realized that my experiences with her gave me a lot to go on in terms of what was important to her."

"So you anticipated how she might act and react. Good."

"Because I know she values a lot of facts and figures, and Red-Greens are all about strategy and fairness, I came into that conference call with all the right data and a foolproof strategy that would appeal to her. I knew she couldn't resist a plan that would be equitable to both of us."

"And did it work?"

"Like a charm," said John, proudly.

"So you respected her motivational value system and delivered *your* message in *her* language. And that prevented conflict from happening?" asked Mac.

"I think she was taken a little off-guard at first; we've done this dance before. She seemed a little cautious there for a minute. But after we started rolling, all was well. A few times, I had to bite my tongue and resist the temptation to go into conflict. She has a way of pushing my buttons."

"And were you successful in not accepting that invitation to conflict?" asked Mac, expectantly.

John smiled, "I hung up on it like a telemarketer at suppertime."

"Excellent. So you were able to identify the early signs of conflict and manage yourself and her through them."

"I guess so, yes. It was amazing. I'd had negotiations with her four other times, and this time—it just... I don't know..."

"It was *nice*," exclaimed Mac with a broad smile.

"Yes, it was nice," said John. "But then I went home."

"Uh, oh."

"Not so nice," said John, wincing.

"What did you do?"

"I didn't do anything!"

"Unfortunately, that's the Achilles Heel of the first-stage Green—not doing anything," admitted Mac. "I struggle with it, too. My wife says it's a disease. She calls it 'deer in the headlights-itis.'"

"I literally walked in the door, and Nancy was on me. I heard the kids crying and immediately knew that the day hadn't gone well for her. I could hear it in the tone of her voice. I knew she was in conflict, but I just choked."

John stood up and started pacing.

"One minute I feel like I'm really getting all this, and then the next, I'm falling flat on my face," said John, with a tinge of desperation.

"OK, but these are two completely different situations."

"But I want to have good outcomes consistently."

"Of course you do. But you can't compare these two instances and get down on yourself. Don't you see how they differ?" asked Mac.

"One was home, and one was work?"

"It's about knowing the people you are in a relationship with well enough to know what's important to them—know what gives them self-worth and how they prefer to operate. Then, you're better prepared to respond to them quickly and effectively. In our last meeting, we made an educated guess that Nancy hails from the nurturing Blue corner of the triangle. Did you keep that in mind when you walked through the door?"

"No. I pretty much just mentally ran away," admitted John.

"I want you to begin asking yourself how people with different motivational values would view a situation and to consider their conflict triggers. If you can do that, you're likely to use a different approach and avoid pulling those triggers."

"Conflict triggers?" asked John.

"Remember, people go into conflict about things that are important to them—values that are tied to their sense of self-worth. So part of anticipating conflict is having a sense of what words or actions might threaten someone's self-worth and push them into conflict—their conflict triggers."

"When I think about it like that," reflected John, "I can see exactly what triggered Nancy's conflict last night. Emma was crying about everything because she didn't have a nap. Nancy wanted to do something to help her feel better, but Emma just needed to go to bed, and she hadn't had her dinner yet. On top of that, J.J. was strug-

powers of inquiry and observation to assess who you're dealing with."

"I don't think I have those powers." said John, with a hint of sarcasm.

"You can develop them."

"How?"

"Think about when we started working together—before we really got into all this—I asked you what was important to you, what kind of environment you found most rewarding. You had no problem finding answers for those questions."

"True."

"You were pretty quick to know what drove you crazy and why."

"And that means what?" asked John.

"Well, how would someone you had a relationship with—a coworker, a boss, a friend, even your wife—know those things about you?"

"If that person was observant, I guess they would pick up on a lot of it," said John. "But the easiest way would be to just ask me."

"That's inquiry and observation," said Mac. "How often are you asking questions like that?"

"Like 'What's your motivation?'"

"Well it can be more subtle than that. Keep in mind, motivation is all about *why*. Why is that important to you? Why do you like working here? Why does that bug you? And then listen carefully for the reasons. The reasons will guide you right to the heart of what people value. And what you hear from a Blue will often sound very different than what you hear from a Green or a Red or someone in the Hub, like me."

"I can imagine. But how do you do it and make it seem natural."

"Well first off, it *should* become natural. Being in relationship with someone should be about really knowing that person—respecting and valuing that person," said Mac. "And the fact is, people generally like talking about themselves."

"So it's not just me?" said John with a smirk.

"The next time you meet someone, get to know them—don't just Rolodex them. People are so much more than a name and place of business. Find out who they are. You'll instantly light a spark of closeness that you may never have experienced before in a 20 second exchange."

"Get to know them in 20 seconds?"

"You don't need their life story. Just figure out what language they're speaking. It's amazing the difference you'll notice immediately. Both of you will feel it."

"OK. I can do that."

"All right. Prove it," said Mac with a mischievous smile.

"Is that a challenge?" asked John.

"See those two guys down there?" Mac pointed down the pier, where two fishermen stood side-by-side, tending a row of fishing rods. "Go have a quick chat and come back and tell me what you think their motivational value system is."

"Seriously? What do I talk to them about?"

"Doesn't matter. Just meet them and practice inquiry and observation."

"OK, fine. I'll do it," said John, sizing them up.

"Oh, but you only have a few minutes. We've still got work to do here," said Mac, as he launched John's new hook out into the water—another perfect cast.

* * *

John was closing in on the two men quickly before realizing he might not get anywhere if they mistook him for some nut job; the pinstripe shirt and slacks were already working against him. So he slowed to a more casual pace and stuck his hands in his pocket.

He looked the two men over to see if there might be clues in their appearance. The older man had a large brace on his left knee. He was dressed more warmly than he needed to be—perhaps he had been here since dawn. Curly, gray hair peeked out from under his cap. The other man was shorter and stockier—probably around 30 years old. He was dressed in a camouflage t-shirt and jeans.

He could hear they were chatting, and they burst into laughter as John reached the railing beside them. John looked back at Mac, who gave him the thumbs up.

John had to chuckle to himself at how silly this felt. It reminded him of approaching some girl at a night club—his buddies back at the table, cheering him on.

He guessed it was time for his pick-up line, "Having any luck out here?"

The two men turned, noticing John for the first time. The older man spoke first, "Not too bad. A few bass."

"We've been using squid," said John, trying to sound like he knew what he was talking about. "Haven't gotten a bite."

"Try mackerel or bunker," said the younger man.

"Oh, yeah?"

"I got plenty of mackerel if you need some," offered the older man.

"Maybe. Thanks," said John, starting to worry that the conversation was becoming too much about fish.

"You always fish in your Sunday best?" asked the younger man.

"Ha. No, I was just meeting a friend out here on my lunch break. I'm a bit of a novice behind a reel."

"It's a great hobby," said the younger man.

"What do you like about it?" asked John, fishing for some motivational clues.

"Fishing? I like the whole process. Picking just the right spot. Picking the lures. Plus, my five kids hate it. It's my own little vacation out of the house—just me and my thoughts."

John was pretty sure those sounded like Green reasons. He figured he'd float some verbal bait and see if he was right.

"I'm guessing you do your homework," said John. "Check the tide schedules, know what's biting when?"

The younger man just smiled and removed a folded wad of papers from his back pocket, "What do you want to know?"

Bingo, John thought. He looked to the older man, "How about you? What brings you out here—besides this amazing weather?"

"I'm here for the fish!" the old man said, proudly.

"And to talk my ear off," said the younger man.

"So you're in it for the sport?" asked John, testing for Red.

"No, I'm really here for the fish. Got a family to take care of. Broke my leg, and they put me on disability, but it's peanuts compared to what I was making at the plant. The wife picked up another shift, but I'm still gonna do whatever it takes to help where I can."

Now, John was thinking perhaps a Red-Blue blend. He tested the water, "So you're here because you want to actively do your part to help your family."

"I'm of no use sitting on my big behind watching *People's Court*. And the fish don't seem to care I got a bum leg."

"Makes sense to me," said John. "Well I'll let you get back to it."

"Hey, when you're ready to learn how to fish like a

pro, I'm here most days," offered the older man.

"I just might take you up on that," said John. "Have a good rest of your day."

John strutted back to Mac, a toothy smile on his face.

"Success?" asked Mac.

"Old guy's a Red-Blue, and the younger guy's a Green."

"Is that right? And how do you know?"

"Old guy's working hard to help his family, and the young guy's all about the process."

"So let's assume you got those reasons right. Do you necessarily know their motivational value system?"

"Sure, it was easy, and kinda fun." John said, proudly.

Mac laughed. "I guess for you I turned getting to know people into a game—a challenge. But I want to caution you here. You made a good first step, but it's important not to make judgments about people too quickly. You got clues from each of them by asking questions that elicited reasons—or motives—in the answer. But remember, a motivational value system is a pattern of motives, and every person has some of every color. Even you sometimes do things for reasons that might sound Blue or Green, right?"

"I suppose that's true," said John. "For the record, I did get more than one reason from each of them."

"And you may be absolutely right about them. But it takes more than a couple data points to show a trend."

"So I may know the reason they are here fishing today," said John, "but I still don't really know their whole motivational value system?"

"Not with certainty," said Mac.

"Then what's the point?"

"It's more than you knew five minutes ago. And it's a very important start—one that will, no doubt, improve your communication choices moving forward," explained Mac. "I'm just cautioning you not to be so quick to declare that you know a person's motivational value system."

"Heck, I don't even know their names. But I know I'm right about those guys. I nailed it," said John with a confident grin.

Mac laughed. "OK, John."

"The Red in me just wishes there was some kind of reward."

"How about I buy you a snow cone?" offered Mac, motioning to the snow cone cart by the edge of the beach.

John laughed, "Deal."

Mac began reeling in his line.

* * *

In his bare feet, John tried to navigate around the small rocks that slowed his progress across the sand. This was accomplished while attempting to eat his lime snow cone with his dress shoes and socks pinned under his arm. Mac trudged on a few steps ahead.

"Anticipating conflict starts with knowing who

you're dealing with," said Mac. "Then you have to ask yourself how people with different motivational values might view a situation. When two or more people see things differently, there is the potential for conflict. If you can figure that out, you have a good shot at steering clear of it."

"OK, let's say I can see a potential conflict coming. How do I stop it?"

"That's when it's time to take action to *prevent* conflict—the second key."

Mac found a suitable spot on the beach and plopped down next to his coolers and fishing poles. John stood there, looking at his suit and shoes and wondering if they'd be salvageable after the beating they'd taken. With a sigh, he tossed them onto the sand and sat down next to Mac.

"Anticipating is something you do in your head, but preventing is where the rubber meets the road. In your conference call with Bonnie, you figured out what part of the triangle she hailed from and prepared yourself. When that call began, you had to put all that anticipation into action. So tell me—knowing that she was a Red-Green, how did you modify your behavior to prevent conflict?"

"Obviously, Red is easy for me, so I just had to act a little more Green than I'm used to. I slowed everything down and acknowledged her role as a good steward of her company's resources. From there, I methodically walked through our service record and the competitive landscape. I tried to stay calm and listen to all her concerns. And when she raised objections, I think I was able to give a firm but logical response."

"Based on your top strengths, I'd say you had to rummage through some of the deeper drawers in your tool box to pull that off."

"I guess I did, and it wasn't always easy. But I knew I had to somehow keep her on board without giving away the store."

"What you did there so adeptly is what we call *borrowing*. It's choosing a non-preferred behavior to achieve a result that is productive in a relationship."

"By 'non-preferred,' do you mean those strengths from the middle drawers in your tool box?"

"Yes. Effective borrowing typically comes out of those middle strengths—not too high or too low on your chart. They are behaviors you can call on in a pinch to get the job done right. In your call with Bonnie, you eased up on the *competitive* and the *ambitious* and brought out the *methodical* and *reserved*."

"Yeah, I guess I knew that if I jumped into a hard sell and made it a competition about price haggling, the whole conversation would spiral down pretty fast," said John.

"By borrowing, you had more productive communication and a better business result—and that's what it's all about."

"It sure felt good," added John. "After the call, Blake, my salesman, was so blown away by how great it had gone, he asked me to coach him."

"Fluid, productive communication can feel pretty fantastic. The key to preventing conflict is figuring out how to get your intent across in a way that they can relate to and in a way that won't be misinterpreted. You do that by borrowing—like you did with Bonnie—but you also do that by using your top strengths appropriately."

"Like not overdoing a strength," recalled John.

"Exactly. If people misperceive or misinterpret what you're doing because you're misusing a strength, then your communication is tainted. Your intent is lost, and the potential for conflict rises."

"What if you don't even realize you're overdoing the strength?" asked John.

"If you can anticipate how a person may interpret your strengths, you can take steps to prevent it coming across as overdone."

"Like with Gail," said John. "She values being cautious and thinking things through. So I need to be careful with my *quick to act* strength around her."

"Yes. You can prevent a lot of conflict with her just by regulating the volume on that one. It's a behavior that's probably a real conflict trigger for her because acting quickly pushes her to operate way out of her comfort zone."

"Let me see if I've got it," said John. "Preventing conflict is really all about the deliberate, appropriate use of strengths in your relationships."

"Exactly," said Mac, proudly. "Anticipating and Preventing conflict are strategies to attempt a pre-emptive strike on conflict. A well-chosen behavior on your part can prevent conflict with another person. But you need to prevent conflict in yourself sometimes, too – and that might have more to do with choosing your perceptions than choosing your behaviors. However, even our best efforts can fail. There will be times where your self-worth is threatened and accepting that invitation is inevitable for yourself or someone else. That's why it's important to get better at *identifying* conflict."

"Yeah, that's an important one," said John. "I seem to be missing the signs with Nancy and not realizing she's there until it's too late."

"Exactly. You're not recognizing her conflict until she's risen to stage two Red. And trust me, John, you will have a much better outcome if you can deal with the conflict in stage one."

"I'll sleep better, too," said John, rubbing his sore neck.

"So it's critical to learn to spot the three basic approaches taken in conflict: the Blue accommodating, the Red rising to the challenge, or the Green cautious analysis. And these approaches can be arranged in any sequence for a person."

"How can you tell what stage they're in?" asked John.

"Chances are you won't—at least not until you've truly mastered the nuances of all this. While it's best to address conflict in stage one—unless you know someone well or know their inventory results—you probably won't know if you're witnessing the first or second-stage of a color. The conflict sequence is going to show up in different ways for different people. So the most helpful advice is to learn to identify all the different colors of conflict."

"It seems like Red is the easiest one to spot," said John.

"I'd say that's true," agreed Mac. "Mainly because it's the most unrestrained and vocal approach. People who use Red first would say they're just rising to the challenge being offered."

John thought of Randy urging him to push back and get tough with Bonnie during the negotiation. Randy was never one to back down when someone challenged him.

"Green, you know because you live it," continued Mac. "People who use Green first want to step back, be cautious, and make sense of it all. They get quiet or demand facts or examples."

"Yep, that's me," agreed John. "I guess the one I'm really struggling with is Blue. If Nancy is a Blue when everything is fine, what do I look for to distinguish whether she's slipped into conflict?"

"People who initially use a Blue approach would

probably say they are trying to keep the peace and accommodate the needs of others. They want to smooth things over."

"I get that, but it's just so subtle," said John, discouraged.

"Remember, you're looking for a shift. Even someone moving from a Blue motivational value system to Blue conflict will show a subtle shift. You need to look for the clues. With Blue, they may start to fidget, clear their throat, or some other sign of discomfort. They'll sometimes sit back and hope others will take care of the issue, so they don't have to face it. You'll often see someone in Blue conflict feeling bad or accepting the blame. And they don't want to fuel the fire, so they stop sharing how they feel. Now, there's a clue for you."

"How so?"

"When things are going well, is Nancy shy about sharing her feelings with you?" asked Mac.

"No."

"There you go. Ask a person in Blue first-stage conflict if they're OK and you'll start getting short, canned answers like, 'Oh, no, I'm fine,' or 'No problem.' Conflict makes them uncomfortable so they go from freely sharing to wanting to direct attention elsewhere."

"Wow," said John. "When you say it like that, she has been giving me plenty of warning signs. I think I've been missing them for a very long time."

"But now you know what to look for. Spotting the

shift in motivation and those subtle clues of conflict is especially difficult with someone like Nancy whose conflict color is so close to their motivational value system. But by raising your awareness and successfully spotting it in stage one, you can avoid the pain and suffering of stage two or three."

"My boss, Gail, has a pretty good poker face, too," said John. "Sometimes I don't know how she feels about what I'm doing. Happy or mad, she's a blank screen. It's not until later that it comes out that something I did or said really bothered her. I'm blindsided."

"It goes back to gaining that understanding of what motivates the person, what their values and priorities are. Of course, you have to answer those questions for yourself as well. And only then can you identify where there could be a clash in styles. You'll have anticipated and identified conflict, even with people who don't show much change."

"I suppose I could just ask if something is bothering her," said John, as if struck by the obvious.

Mac looked over at him and smiled, "Asking sincere and appropriate questions with the intent of preventing or managing conflict is almost never a bad idea."

John was staring out at the ocean as a wave crashed louder than he had noticed before. The two men watched as the water pushed forward toward their spot with unrestrained force. John looked over at Mac, who didn't flinch. John readied for a quick retreat but the creeping water stopped three-feet from their feet and receded as quickly as it had approached.

"Tide's coming in," said Mac. "Why don't we pick this up later."

Mac stood and brushed the sand off. John glanced at his notepad.

"What about *Manage* conflict and *Resolve* conflict?" asked John. His own voice reminded him of his daughter's—as if pleading for another ride on the carousel.

"Oh, those are good ones."

"You're going to leave me hanging?"

"I'm going to leave you with some advice, John," said Mac, picking up his fishing equipment. "From one first-stage Green husband to another... call your wife and apologize about last night. I don't know how much you've told her about the work we're doing together, but she might be less upset if she understood how you process conflict. You don't want her continuing to think you're this cold, uncaring guy—because you're not."

They were simple words, but the sincerity in Mac's eyes warmed John to his core. They energized him, and the dread he felt about going home that evening had been replaced by anticipation. He turned and saw that Mac was now already halfway to the street. "Thanks, Mac!" John called out.

Mac turned and acknowledged him with a smile.

EIGHT

"You bought new clothes," observed Nancy, as she sipped from her glass of wine.

"Yeah, my other ones smelled like Fisherman's Wharf," said John.

Nancy's eyebrows furrowed as she laughed. "What? Why?"

"Long story."

John had, in fact, headed straight to the mall after leaving the beach. The reservation for their favorite restaurant had been made in the car, and—for the first time ever—he had bought roses from a man with a bucket on the side of the road. He realized the whole "flowers-in-hand apology" was a bit cliché. But the fact that John had never actually done it himself gave it a flair of originality. At least, that's how he rationalized it.

"You were able to get the kids covered?" asked John.

"Yeah, my mom came over."

John nodded and drained the last sip from his own glass of wine. He sensed an awkwardness that proved the dust had yet to settle between them, despite his uncharacteristic attempt at chivalry. He felt the heavy weight of Green conflict tugging on his thoughts. He considered excusing himself for a trip to the restroom but fought back the urge—determined to take action. After all, it was why he convened this meeting.

"I suppose we should talk about last night," said John.

"Look, I'm sorry about how I acted," said Nancy, striking first.

"No. You have no need to apologize. This is my apology."

"Are we going to fight over who gets to apologize?" Nancy smiled.

"How sad would that be?"

"Very. Anyway, I shouldn't have jumped down your throat the second you walked in the door. It wasn't very considerate on my part."

"Well I realize the day had been kind of a disaster for you," said John. "I could have handled it a lot better. I want you to know I'm really working on that."

"I know you are," said Nancy, as she raised her glass. "And I accept your apology."

John finished refilling his glass from the bottle chilling in the stand next to their table. He met his glass with hers in a toast.

"And I, yours."

Nancy pulled back her glass, mid-sip.

"Oh! I almost forgot. I have some good news!"

"What kind of news?"

"I received my first signed contract today. A big free-lance gig with that non-profit I was telling you about."

"Really? Congratulations!" said John, as they re-clinked their glasses. "How much?"

"How much? You mean money? I don't know. Enough."

John could sense the annoyance building in her words. Money may have been a motivator for him but never for her. He mentally put his Blue glasses on and tried to dig his way back out.

"Sorry," said John. "You know me—all about the ne-gotiation. That's wonderful news, Nancy. You're so good at helping people, and I know how much it means to you to get back out there."

"Yeah, it'll be nice being of service to someone who actually values what I can do for them. The kids sure don't."

"Oh, that's not true. Whether they say it or not, they appreciate all that you do. We all do. You're amazing."

"Thanks," said Nancy with a heartfelt smile.

"When do you start?"

"Monday," she said with a tinge of dread. "It's going to keep me pretty busy over the next three weeks."

Nancy must have seen behind John's smile, as he assessed what that would mean for him in terms of carting the kids around and being home on time.

"We talked about this," she reminded him.

"I know. It's fine. I'm genuinely happy for you."

"I can have my mother help out more."

"No, I got it," said John. "You do so much for me and the kids, the least I can do is give you an opportunity to do something for yourself."

Nancy tilted her head and grinned, "OK, who are you and what have you done with my husband?"

"What?" asked John, innocently.

"You're being so..."

"Mooshy?"

"I was gonna say 'Perfect.' Is Cyrano de Bergerac sitting behind you?"

"I've just been learning a lot about how I can be managing my relationships better."

"I thought these meetings were all about conflict."

"Well, yes. They're about managing conflict," said John, "but they're also about preventing it altogether. And that starts with knowing the people in my life better and interacting with them in a more productive way. The best way to deal with conflict is never having to get there in the first place."

"Well you've made quite an 'about face' since last night."

"It's really starting to click for me. Dr. Mac is helping me understand that the way I see the world can be pretty different than how you see it or how Gail sees it."

"And how do you see it?"

"I'm a Red—an Assertive-Directing—which means I'm usually focused on tasks, getting the job done, and getting results. It also means that I like challenging, fast-moving, and competitive environments, where I have the opportunity for recognition and advancement."

"Well that explains why you're taking this missed promotion so hard."

"Yeah. That job was really important to me. I value success, and I work hard to get it. When I didn't get the promotion, it felt like my values were being threatened."

"But you still have your family and friends, a good job, nice house—you have a lot to be thankful for. There'll be other promotions."

"And you're absolutely right. But see, you don't value those Red things like results and task-accomplishment the way I do, so it's harder for you to understand why it tore me up the way that it did."

"So what do I value?" asked Nancy.

"Well, you'll need to take the inventory," said John with a smile. "But I have my guesses."

"Based on how you've laid it on so far tonight, I'd say you've guessed right."

John smiled. "You're my true Blue, honey. Motivated by helping and protecting other people. You want to help make a difference in people's lives... hence you giving away your talent to that non-profit."

"Hey, I'm making money," said Nancy, playfully.

"Does my assessment sound right to you?" asked John.

"Duh," offered Nancy in agreement.

"So a lot of times, those differences between you and me can get us into trouble if we don't quite understand them. Before I started all this, I just assumed you saw the world the same way I did, and as a result, I sometimes saw your behavior as weird or counterproductive and got really frustrated by it."

"So now you understand me better?"

"I'm not just understanding you—I'm respecting the way you see things. This stuff really helps you value what people are bringing to the table."

"Sounds like really amazing work you're doing, John."

"And I haven't even gotten to the conflict sequence."

"Conflict is a sequence?"

John nodded. "In three stages. And it reveals how people change their motivation and behavior during conflict. We're just trying to protect what's important to us and work our way back to a place where we feel good about ourselves."

"OK, wow. You lost me," said Nancy.

"Remember the way I reacted last night when I came in the door?"

"You didn't react at all. You just stood there."

"Exactly. Did that look like a man who's a hard-charging Red?"

"Not at all."

"Because in the face of conflict, I changed."

"Into a statue?"

John laughed. "Maybe I looked like a statue, but that was my first-stage Green conflict. For me, I deal with conflict by needing to step back and think it through. It's a very analytical process that happens to me."

Nancy considered that for a moment. "That totally makes sense. You've always kind of shut down or run away."

"But only because I need a minute to process it all. It's not hiding; it's preparing."

"I never considered that," said Nancy.

"Because in the past we haven't understood how we're different, it's led to conflict between us. As we start to understand and appreciate how differently we operate, I think we could have an even better relationship and spend less time in conflict."

"I love the sound of that," said Nancy.

"And this is going to help me in all of my relationships—both at work and home."

"So what do I do in conflict?" Now, she was testing him.

"I used to think you went Red first—ready to start swinging. But as I've learned more about how conflict works, I'm pretty sure Red is your second-stage of conflict. You initially go Blue in conflict."

"Which means what?"

"You accommodate—try to keep the peace."

"Well, a lot of conflict is just not worth getting into," she said defensively. "I just want to smooth things over so we can move on."

"See? I'm right! First-stage Blue," exclaimed John.

"OK, congratulations, smart guy."

"Sorry. I've just been screwing this up for so long I'm kind of excited to start getting it right. Things are going to be a whole lot better, I think."

"I think so, too," said Nancy, raising her glass.

"If we keep toasting, we're going to need to order another bottle of wine," said John, smiling broadly.

* * *

"Knock, knock," said John, as he stuck his head into Gail's office. "Is now still a good time?"

Gail swiveled away from her computer screen and peered at him over her glasses, "Sure, John. You're right on time. Have a seat."

John settled into one of the guest chairs in front of Gail's desk and placed a file folder within reach on the empty chair next to him. He had started training himself to picture a colored glow around people as he interacted with them. Currently, Gail's tight hair bun was radiating a thick, Green halo. It was a silly game he played, but so far, it was working for him.

"I appreciate you making time for me today," said

John. "I know our weekly check-in is normally on Friday, but I wanted to provide some info on a new opportunity I've been cultivating. I thought I should give you some time with the data before our meeting at the end of the week."

"Sounds good. Let's see what you have."

"Great," he said, as he grabbed the folder. "There's a lot of moving parts with this one, so please feel free to stop me if you have any questions or if I miss something."

"Alright."

"So a couple weeks ago, I was finally able to meet with Roger Hutchins, the COO at Ambrose Industries."

"Really," said Gail, shifting forward in her seat, "We've been trying to get in front of Hutchins for almost two years."

"I know. I was starting to think he didn't actually exist," said John. "To be fair, Lisa Meyer, my new rep who works the Ambrose account has done a great job networking with some key people, and she deserves the credit. Lisa invited me to be part of the meeting with Mr. Hutchins when all of the pieces fell into place."

"Lisa Meyer, huh? Bring in a copy of her resume on Friday," said Gail, intrigued by the potential of a new rising star. "How did your meeting go?"

John smiled. He was instantly struck with the urge to boast about his expert handling of Hutchins. He'd been in rare form that day, and the negotiation had been perfect. It was all John could do to keep from jumping straight to the outcome. But there was that big green glow reminding him to stick to the plan—keep it nice and organized.

"Well, the meeting lasted over an hour, but the short version is, he's open to using our products exclusively, if we're willing to partner with them on a new marketing campaign and share in the development costs associated with integrating our new components. I don't think I have to tell you how big this is. If we're willing to come to the table, I think he'll move forward with us."

John watched as Gail just sat there, slowly nodding. Against his better judgment, he couldn't resist adding one little Red starburst to the pitch, "This could be a *game changer* for both companies."

"It sounds promising, but there are a lot of details to consider—a lot of questions to be answered. I hope you don't expect an answer from me today, because this is going to take some pretty detailed analysis."

John realized he was at the conflict crossroads. Of course he wanted an answer right away, but if he pushed Gail into conflict, this deal might never get done. He took a deep breath and wrestled his *quick to act* back into his tool belt.

"I completely understand. There's a lot of complexity with this one, and we'd be crazy not to do our homework and make sure we can justify the investment. I've already begun looking at the numbers, and I'd like to share some of the research I've started. I'm hoping you can let me know what questions I still should be asking. Then we can regroup on Friday."

"When is Ambrose expecting an answer?" asked Gail.

"I told Mr. Hutchins that we would need to do our due diligence, and he agreed. We're not meeting again until next month. In the meantime, he gave me access to his key operations and marketing guys for ongoing dialogue. It looks like they're going to be pretty open with their information."

"That's good, John. If we have that kind of access, we should be able to make an informed decision in that amount of time. Where are you on the research?"

John handed her a thin, spiral bound document.

"I had Jane in Business Analytics run a forecast using four different scenarios. The one that looks best to me is on top, and the other three follow. Leslie in Marketing helped me with the business case. You'll see that the marketing spend is outlined in section two, along with detailed budgets for the campaign. Their guys, I'm sure, will want to chime in, but I think we've given them a good starting point. At least enough to make a conservative estimation of our costs."

Gail leaned back in her chair, her head already buried in the data. After a thick silence where John could swear he heard his own pulse, she peeked over the top of the document.

"We may want to talk to legal."

"I thought so, too," said John, hiding a smile. "Our associate counsel is reviewing it and promised to e-mail us his opinion in advance of our Friday meeting."

Gail closed the document and placed it squarely on her desk.

"I have to say, John, I am thoroughly impressed."

"With my research or the fact that I was able to wait two weeks before telling you I got to Hutchins?" said John smiling.

"Both," said Gail. "And frankly, your timing couldn't be more opportune." Her voice grew quiet as she glanced out the door. "There's a rumor that the new Chairman of the Board might be showing up for an ambush sometime soon."

"Philip Keyes is coming here? Should I be worried?"

"We all should be. He's been getting pretty vocal about his displeasure with this division of the corporation. I think he's coming in to shake things up. It's anyone's guess what that might mean."

John felt the Green wave of first-stage conflict crash over him. Keyes had recently bought enough shares of Starr to secure himself a position on the board and had quickly become elected chairman. Keyes was notorious for walking into the companies his corporation owned and wreaking havoc. A cost cutter, ruthless, vindictive, watch what you say, don't get noticed... avoid at all costs. He was rumored to have visited one company and ordered everyone on even-numbered floors laid off. John knew that as word of Keyes' visit spread through the halls of Starr Industries, conflict was going to surge from every corner of the building.

NINE

B OILED, FRIED, OR SCRAMBLED?" asked the bubbly twenty something waitress.

"It's anyone's guess," sighed John.

"Come again?" she asked, befuddled.

"Don't mind him," said Mac. "He's in conflict."

"Oh," she said, staring blankly. "Why don't I give you all another minute."

"Thanks," said Mac.

The bright morning sun streamed in through the windows of the non-descript downtown diner. John was wishing he had his sunglasses, as he stared blankly at the moving shadow produced by the coffee cup he rotated on the table.

"You don't even know if anything's going to happen," said Mac.

"It doesn't matter. Everyone is freaking out anyway."

"Good time to test your skills."

"Skills..." said John, gloomily. "Why does it feel like you taught me the dog paddle, and now, I'm being thrown into the middle of the ocean?"

"Believe me, John. You're practically a triathlete. Look at what you've already been able to do in your relationships at work and at home."

"I know. I guess I'm just feeling a little..."

"Green?" suggested Mac. "You could use this opportunity to be a real example for your coworkers. How far would that go toward changing any lingering misperceptions of you?"

John finally looked up from his coffee.

"Look, don't worry," reassured Mac. "Today is all about navigating conflict that already exists. We've looked at how to prevent it and identify it. Now we'll take on *managing* it."

John exhaled deeply.

"You're going to come out of this diner a master," promised Mac. "But first, you have to come back."

"Come back from where?" asked John, wearily.

"Your cave. Or whatever dark place you go in Green conflict. I need you present. We're not going to get anywhere with you in conflict. When we're stuck in a place of protecting our self-worth, it's much harder to help others protect or restore what's important to them. And that's the primary mission of managing conflict."

"Helping them out of conflict?"

"Not quite. Managing conflict is about creating the

conditions that empower others to manage themselves out of their emotional state of conflict. It's also about managing yourself out. What I'm asking of you right now is what you need to be able to do later."

"You can't rescue someone who's drowning when you're drowning too. Is that the idea?" asked John.

"Exactly! To effectively manage conflict, we have to begin with ourselves," Mac made a fist and hit his chest, producing two dull thuds. "It starts right here. If we're pulled into conflict ourselves, we're usually not in a great position to help others."

"I think I scared the waitress away," said John.

Mac gave her a wave from across the restaurant.

"Like most everything we've talked about," said Mac, "it's a choice. As soon as we know what's happening under the hood, we have to take responsibility for it. If you're feeling the conflict right now, just choose out of it."

"Simple as that?"

"You're in charge, remember?" Mac smiled. "That's not to say you won't feel that Green shift, but use that first-stage shift like a smoke alarm—an alert system. If you were sitting in your house and the smoke detector went off, would you keep sitting there, or would you take some sort of action?"

"Action," said John.

"And that action would depend on the situation. Is the toast burning, or is the whole kitchen on fire? Do you open a window, or do you run outside and call for help? When you stop letting conflict control you, you'll hear that alarm sooner, and you'll be prepared to respond appropriately."

John smiled at the visual Mac had so vividly painted. The truth was, he had often found himself sitting in the smoke of his own "burnt toast," while other people wondered if he was going to do something about it. He wondered why he was willing to put himself through something so unpleasant and unproductive.

The waitress reappeared at their table.

"Hi," she said, cheerily. "All better?"

"Much," said John.

After ordering breakfast and getting his coffee topped off, John received a text on his cell phone. He shook his head as he read it.

Deep breath, John, he said to himself.

"What's going on?" asked Mac.

"Oh, nothing. I have this one rep who feels he needs to run every little thing by me."

"Now, besides taking a deep breath, what else can you do to keep from letting that bother you about him?"

"Besides leaving my phone in the car?" said John grinning.

"Yes, besides complete avoidance of the relationship."

"Well—like you suggested a few weeks ago about things I find annoying—look for the strength at play behind the behavior."

"Great one. Managing yourself in conflict can be as easy as taking some time to see things differently. When you do that, you can start to understand, and perhaps even appreciate, another person's motives. Why do you think your rep is contacting you so much?"

"I don't think he likes the isolation of being out on the road. He's a pretty social guy—always coming up with an endless list of options for his customers. If I had to guess, I'd say he's a Hub."

"So a Flexible-Cohering like me," said Mac. "What's the strength he's overdoing?"

"Indecisive? He wants to be so flexible and open to ideas that he seems to find it impossible to make a decision."

"To him, being flexible, and part of a cohesive, interactive group brings him self-worth."

"There are definitely worse things, I guess," said John.

"Certainly not worth getting into conflict over. When you take the time to get to know a person at a level where you understand their motives, their values, and their sources of self-worth and esteem, you are less likely to find yourself in conflict. It's hard to dislike a person that you know."

"And by 'know,' you mean know their motivational value system?" asked John.

"Yes. Just understand them. Know where they're coming from."

The waitress returned with their orders. "Here we go,

boys."

"Thank you," said Mac.

John studied the waitress as she placed his eggs in front of him. "You seem to enjoy your work. What's your favorite part?"

"Of working here?" she asked. "Well I'm working my way through nursing school right now, but I suppose I just like being around people. You meet so many different kinda people in a place like this. It's fun, I guess."

"Cool," said John.

Mac snuck John a wink.

"Enjoy!" she said. "Let me know if you need anything."

With that, she was gone.

As John said, "Blue," he heard Mac say, "Hub."

"Looks like we have a difference of opinion," noted Mac. "What 'reason' did you hear?"

"She likes people and wants to be a nurse. Made me think Blue. You?"

"I could see that," said Mac. "What I heard was that she gets to meet a lot of different kinds of people, and that it's fun. As you can see, our filters influence what we see and hear. I might have heard the Hub reason. That sounded best to me."

"So who's right?" asked John.

"It might be a little early in our relationship with Natasha to know for sure."

"Who's Natasha?"

"The Hub waitress," said Mac, with a smirk, "unless she's wearing someone else's name tag."

"Ha! You think you're right!" John accused.

"I'm kidding. But, you know, we could both be right."

"Well, that's no fun."

"It's something to keep in mind. Remember on the stage how the Red, Blue, and Green spotlights blended together? They showed white in the center. Motivational value systems have different shades with no strict borders. Somebody can be clearly in the Blue, *or* their Blue can be a little more flexible—closer to the Hub. Recognizing a person's motivational value system is a fine art. We can start by looking for one of the seven types, but as we learn more, we can fine-tune our understanding to notice when people are on the border between two types. We can tell if someone's Blue motivational values also have a bit of assertive Red, analytical Green or flexible Hub mixed in."

"So the triangle is really just a New York loft apartment," said John.

Mac cocked his head and smiled, "How so?"

"There's no walls. One corner is the bedroom area, while another corner is the family room area. You recognize the differences between them, but the exact point where one room ends and the other one begins is kinda fuzzy."

"OK, sure," said Mac, laughing. "The triangle is a big loft apartment. Now where were we?"

"The Blue waitress," said John.

"No, that was just one of my Hub tangents. We're here to talk about managing conflict."

"Oh, right. That," sighed John, remembering the doom and gloom pervading his office right now.

"Managing conflict has two components," continued Mac. "Managing yourself and managing the relationship. Managing yourself is about addressing your own feelings in the conflict, discovering what got you there, and finding a path back to your motivational value system. It's about keeping your energy available for the other component—managing the relationship. Then you can create the conditions where the other person can manage themselves."

"What do you mean by, 'create the conditions?'" asked John.

"Knowing a person is in Red, Green, or Blue conflict and respecting that motivation. It means giving them what they need in that moment."

"Like the different ways you handled Mabel and your guitar hero Kraig?"

"Exactly. Even the way I handled you."

"Me?"

"When you arrived on the pier the other day, you were still deep in your first-stage Green about the fight you had with your wife. You may not have noticed it, but I didn't push my agenda for the day. I gave you some space to come around. I let you talk about what was bothering you when you were ready."

"Huh," said John, impressed.

"When people are in the cautious Green conflict state, give them some time or space, if possible. If something needs to be dealt with more urgently, try to set a time for a discussion—even if it's only five minutes away. Is that the way you'd like to be handled when you're in conflict?"

"Absolutely. It's funny—after I know a big shipment has been sent to a customer—if I see a call come in from them, I always let it go to voicemail, just in case something is wrong with the order. I'm not avoiding them necessarily. I just want to hear their message first. I call right back, but even that extra minute helps me feel prepared for the call."

"Hey, whatever it takes to manage yourself," said Mac. "Now when people are in the Blue, accommodating conflict state, it's important to listen, check in with them, and give them several opportunities to express themselves. They really want to smooth it over, so they may say that everything is 'fine.' But asking a second time could help them feel more open to say what's really bothering them—and it shows them you really care. You want to help them avoid bottling it up, because there's only so much 'grinning and bearing it' a person can take."

"When that bottle bursts, you better duck," contributed John from personal experience with Nancy.

Mac nodded. "People in the Red, 'rise to the challenge' state want to be heard out. You'll want to quickly identify any points of agreement and ideally take action—or at least commit to taking action—if appropriate. And if you disagree on how, at least try to get on common ground about the desired outcome."

"It seems like doing all that would be pretty difficult if I'm in my first-stage Green. How can I quickly talk things out with someone in Red conflict if I need a minute to regroup?"

"Again, that's why it's important to get yourself under control and out of conflict, so you can better manage the relationship. Here's what's worked well for me. Take the time to fully listen to their concern—look at it as collecting information. Then ask when a decision needs to be made and agree to talk again at that time. That gives you the time you need to think and lets them know that you're serious about addressing the issue. With practice, it will come more naturally."

"So do your best to meet them where they're at," said John.

"Exactly," said Mac. "Conflict is an emotional state. It's very difficult to get resolution until people's emotional needs are met. Show them you understand where they're at, and approach them based on how they're feeling in the conflict. Find out what's important to them, respect that—and only then should you introduce what's important to you."

"It's like a good sales conversation," said John. "Listen to the client's needs, *and then* talk about what you have to offer that fits their needs."

"That's a good way to look at it. And if it's done well, both parties benefit from the relationship."

'Well that's a conversation I think I could pull off," said John.

"Of course you can," said Mac. "But be careful not to confuse 'ending the conversation' with 'ending the conflict.' If there's a break in the conversation, it might mean that people are still thinking about it—not that the conflict is over."

"When is the conflict over?"

"Well, let's talk about that," said Mac.

"I used to say it was over when I won," said John, grinning. "Is it safe to assume Dr. Mac Wilson doesn't condone that viewpoint?"

"That would be safe to assume, yes," replied Mac. "As excruciating as it may be, we need to avoid the temptation to want to *win* the fight or *beat* the other person. Creating winners and losers in conflict is rarely effective in the long run. In fact, it can lead to more conflict in the future."

"So what then? The old 'win-win' solution?"

"Not really. At least not yet. Win-win is a great goal for negotiation, problem-solving, and other forms of opposition. But because *conflict*, as we've defined it, is an emotional state between people, win-win conceptually falls flat. It doesn't take into account the very real pres-

ence of emotions like anger, fear, helplessness, uncer-
tainty, frustration, isolation... Those emotions must be
worked through before any objective, win-win outcomes
can be addressed."

"Is this where I have to become an armchair thera-
pist?"

"Working through people's emotions can sound
daunting," said Mac, "but if you approach it in the context of everything we've been talking about, it becomes
a little easier. *Resolving* conflict is the fifth and final key
to having a nice conflict. It's the final step in the conflict
journey."

"And where is that journey headed?"

"Home," said Mac.

"Happy place?" asked John.

Mac nodded. "It really boils down to this: To create
movement toward resolution, we need to show the other
person the path back to self-worth."

"Where they feel good about themselves," said John.

"Exactly. Where they're not distracted by the emotions of conflict. That's why the *manage* key is so important. It empowers you to understand the emotions you're
seeing in others and approach them where they are at the
moment; to connect. But to really get resolution, we need
to help them back to self-worth. Two people could have
the same emotional experience in conflict—like you and
Gail both being first-stage Green—but you could have
entirely different motivational value systems—different

destinations on your return-journey."

"In conflict," said John, "we both need time to think and make sense of it all..."

"But you want back to Red, and she wants back to Green. Your path home is different than her path," said Mac.

"What does that mean in terms of what I do in a conflict situation with her?" asked John

"For you, getting conflict resolved means turning that Green thinking and logic into *action*, so you can feel good about yourself. Your Green conflict needs to produce a Red, results-oriented solution. For Gail, her Green conflict needs to produce a Green, methodical and reproducible solution. Even though you often experience similar feelings at the beginning of conflict, the trips back to your respective motivational value systems go to very different places."

"So we won't be on the same flight," said John with a smile.

"Not unless you have a reason to be in Greenland."

John took a large bite of food—mostly so he could absorb what he had just heard. When he got into conflict with Gail, he'd been trying to get her out of it by pushing her where he wanted to go instead of where she wanted to go. She wanted back to Green, but he was dragging her in his direction. As a result, their conflicts went on longer than they needed to.

"This explains a lot," said John. "When Gail and I are

in conflict, I'm trying to make it better, but I'm actually making it worse. What I need to do, instead, is come up with the action-oriented solution that I need but make sure that it's also organized and reproducible. When I come up with an idea to solve a problem for one customer, she always looks at what kind of precedent it sets for how we solve this with other customers."

"Very insightful, John," said Mac. "Now what about other people?"

John's thoughts first went to Nancy. He had always believed that conflict was resolved when she had agreed on an action, a goal, or an outcome. But resolution to Nancy was different. For her, the goal didn't matter so much as the people. Sometimes he would be pushing for a result, and she would say things like *You've got so many things to be thankful for already.* When he dismissed that type of statement, she usually got mad at him, second-stage Red. He was trying to send Nancy down the wrong path and paid for it with escalating conflict.

When his mind returned to work, he thought of Leslie; she didn't like the way he and Randy's competition disrupted the team. She wanted everyone to get along, to collaborate. The path out of conflict for her was all about consensus and getting everyone on the same page. She wanted back to the Hub.

Randy was another story entirely. John rarely had conflict with Randy (though he had learned that other people, like Leslie, saw their treatment of each other during competition as conflict). On the rare occasions when there was conflict between them, it had been easy to resolve, because their path out went to the same place. The journey back to Red meant simply showing the results and—boom—the conflict was over.

Breakfast was soon over, too. John and Mac left the diner and meandered down the bustling city streets.

* * *

"Keep in mind," said Mac. "Resolution is not for one person at the expense of another; it's not 'ending the conversation.' True conflict resolution makes it easier for both people to feel good about themselves and the relationship. It's also important to know that not every conflict is going to get resolved. Part of managing conflict is recognizing when it's time to exit or perhaps even end a relationship."

The comment reminded John that this was to be their last meeting. While he was excited to continue trying out all of the tools that Mac had revealed to him, John began to wonder if he was as ready as Mac seemed to think he was. The unrest at work was weighing on him. And at home, while John and Nancy were seeing positive changes in their communication, it still wasn't as consistent as he would like.

"Can I ask you a personal question?" asked John.

"You can always ask... I'll reserve the right to not answer."

"Good enough. You seem to have it all figured out. I guess you and your wife never have conflict? Picture perfect marriage, right?"

"Not true at all," said Mac. "We still have conflict, but it's less than it used to be. We're able to prevent the majority of it. Some people say that a relationship without conflict is probably a sign that you're not talking about the things that really matter. And they're probably right."

"I'd agree with that," said John.

"Remember that conflict comes from a perceived threat to self-worth, and each person has a unique sense of identity and a unique view of what self-worth looks like to them. No two people have exactly the same values. So it's almost automatic that an important relationship will have some conflict in it. And in that conflict, there is the opportunity to learn about what really matters to you and the other person. To keep a relationship going, you've got to *manage* the conflict so that the threats to self-worth are removed and *resolve* it so the results of the conflict confirm each person's self-worth. That's truly the bottom line of what it means to have a nice conflict."

"Simple as that, huh, Doc?"

"It comes down to making good choices and using our skills to prevent it. And if you can't prevent the conflict, then you have to manage the conflict."

"Like the old saying: If you can't beat 'em, join 'em," said John.

"I guess that's true," said Mac. "If you can't prevent

it, manage it."

In a small park across the street, several pairs of men played chess in the brisk morning sunshine. Mac checked his watch and stopped.

"Do you have a minute? There's someone I'd like you to talk to."

Before John could reply, Mac was dodging cars on his way over to the park.

By the time John had made his way safely across the street, Mac was already seated at one of the concrete tables. Mac waved him over.

"Over here, John," called Mac.

The man sitting opposite Mac turned, and John instantly recognized the glowing, weathered face of Walter Freeman.

"Walter?" asked John, in disbelief.

Walter slowly stood and grasped John's outstretched hand.

"Well, whaddya know?" said Walter. "What a wonderful surprise!"

"For you and me, both," said John.

"Our friend, John, here, has just graduated from our little conflict crash course," said Mac.

"And?" Walter asked John.

"There was a lot of crashing," admitted John. "But it's amazing. I can't begin to tell you what it's already done for me."

"Try."

175

"Well, my boss and I are really starting to click. And things between Nancy and I have never been better."

"Good. You screw things up with that pretty little lady, I'll smack you myself," said Walter with a wink.

"Don't worry," assured John. He motioned to the chess board between them. "You two do this often?"

"Every Friday morning."

"He got tired of me kicking his butt on the golf course," added Mac.

Walter flashed Mac a dirty look and sat back down. "Enough out of you, Theodore."

"That IS your name," exclaimed John, remembering Mabel calling him by the same name.

"Legal name. It's a long story," said Mac, without looking up from the chess pieces he meticulously arranged in front of him.

"Your grandfather really did have a thing for Roosevelt," said John.

"That's true," said Walter. "Should I tell him where the nickname 'Mac' comes from?"

"No," said Mac, trying to hide a smile. "Walter is an old friend of my grandfather's. I've basically known him my whole life."

"I taught him everything he knows," said Walter, grinning. Then his face grew serious. "And he taught me everything I know. The kid knows his stuff." The two men exchanged a look. John felt a sort of father-son warmth between them. Walter smacked the seat beside him, "You gonna stand there all day? Sit down. Get ready for the master class in chess... the game of kings."

"I wanted to thank you again for doing this for me," said John, sincerely, as he slid his legs under the concrete picnic table.

"Bah!" said Walter, swatting at John's words as they hung in the air. "I'd do it for everyone I know if this joker wasn't so busy. I have an easier time getting a table at Le Bernardin."

"Well it means a lot—"

"I know, Johnny. The fact that you actually followed through and stayed with it is all the thanks you owe me."

John smiled at how poorly Walter accepted compliments.

"Now, when you're learning to play chess," continued Walter, "the first thing you have to do is learn the different pieces and how each one moves. The Bishops move diagonally as far as they want, and the Rooks move in straight lines as far as they want. The King and Queen move in any direction, but the King can go only one space, while the Queen—"

"I actually know how to play chess, Walter," interrupted John.

"Hold your horses, sport. You'll never get the point if you don't spend a little time sharpening. May I go on?"

"Please," said John, wondering if his own Red value system could be blamed for his patience deficiency.

"Once you learn the moves," said Walter, "it's easy to

play the game. But to master chess... now, that's another thing entirely. You could play this game your whole life and always find ways to improve. The game gets complicated because it's not really about moving the pieces around at all; it's about the relationships between the pieces and how they accomplish their objective."

Walter's point started to sink in for John. He and Mac shared a look as Walter continued.

"You have to learn to think several steps ahead, to *anticipate* your opponent's moves and *prevent* him from attacking your pieces. You have to be able to *identify* when you are getting into trouble and to *manage* yourself out of that trouble so you can bring the game to a satisfactory *resolution*—winning."

Mac was watching John, "Anything sound familiar?"

"Suspiciously familiar," said John, grinning. He opened his notebook and glanced at his notes. "Anticipate, prevent, identify, manage, and resolve. But I thought conflict shouldn't be about *winning.*"

"Conflict shouldn't, but life should," said Walter.

"Life is won when you achieve the kind of relationships and success you want for yourself," Mac stated.

"I feel like I'm winning the game of life, because I'm living the life I want to live" added Walter. "Did you feel like you were winning when you were struggling at work or fighting with your wife?"

"Quite the opposite," admitted John.

"This chess board," said Mac, "is sort of like our three-color triangle. And on it, Reds, Blues, Greens, Hubs, and the blends are all moving in a predictable way, like the various chess pieces."

"When you understand people's motives," said Walter, "you know what they're likely to do when things are going well and when they're experiencing conflict."

Mac waved his hand over the black chess army in front of him, "And each piece is working together in a unified effort. They're like a work team—a system of personalities working toward a common goal. I'm still fascinated by how people work together and how we can help people and teams become more productive."

"That's interesting," said John staring at the chess pieces. "It made me realize something else. If one person does something, it's going to affect the other people on the team, right? Sometimes, it's positive, but other times, it's negative. So when one person moves into conflict, you can start to anticipate how that might impact the other people in the group—how the conflict could spread throughout the group as they join in the conflict."

"That's very true," said Mac.

"Even the way pieces move... sometimes, the movement of a chess piece is really obvious, and other times, you have to ask the other player, 'Did you move?' That's really true for people, too. Some moves to conflict are really easy to identify, and others are a little harder to notice. Does that make sense?"

"He's already building on your concepts," said Walter

to Mac.

"I told you I'd make him into a master," said Mac.

John wanted to make some self-effacing comment, but the fact was, he was really feeling confident in the tools he had learned over the past few weeks. Perhaps *master* wasn't such an exaggeration after all.

TEN

GOOD MORNING, Gail," said John in a sing-song voice even he didn't recognize.

"You're in a good mood this morning," she said, as she rushed through the entrance door John was holding open for her.

"Yeah, well I almost had a fight with my wife last night."

"OK," said Gail, looking at him perplexed. "That makes no sense whatsoever."

"Emphasis on the word, *almost*," said John, proudly.

"Does this have to do with the work you're doing around conflict?"

"It's amazing," said John, enthusiastically.

His exuberance was met with a hollow look of indifference. John smiled as he noticed the Green glow around her face. He chose some new words. "Real common-sense stuff, but well-researched and tested. I'll get you some info on it."

"I'd be interested to see that."

John pushed the button to hail the elevator for them.

"I'm assuming what you've learned helped you with your argument last night?" she asked.

"Well, that's the great thing. There wasn't one. I was able to prevent the argument before it started."

The elevator doors opened, and they stepped inside, along with a small group of other people.

"Preventing conflict," said John, "is about anticipating it, then actively averting it by either changing your perception or changing your behavior."

John recognized the discomfort in Gail's eyes and smiled to himself. To Gail, the topic was clearly "too personal" for a crowded elevator. He remembered Gail admonishing him in the past for continuing conversations during the long ride to their floor. She was an intensely private person—a trait John figured fit nicely with her autonomous Green motivational values. John stopped talking; if it made Gail uncomfortable, news of his victory on the home front could wait until later.

* * *

"You're out of line!" boomed Randy's voice, as John and Gail approached the meeting room.

Through the glass walls, John could see Randy towering over the large crowd of executives seated around the conference table. *Uh, oh,* John thought. *Here we go.*

John's good mood circled the drain and disappeared, as he was reminded of the dark cloud that had been hanging over the staff for days. People were on edge. Tempers had been flaring—all because of a rumor about the mysterious and dreaded Philip Keyes being in town.

John walked inside the room and could instantly feel he was entering the epicenter of conflict at Starr Industries. He fought off the urge to turn and walk out. This room was to be his prison for the next two days, as the annual 'show and tell' with the vice president was about to kick off. It was the key sales meeting of the year, and all five regional sales directors and all 40 sales managers were required to attend. It appeared that everyone was already here, so Randy had ample audience for his outburst.

"Just calm down," said Leslie, crossing her arms and glaring.

"Calm down? You're screwing with our livelihoods," yelled Randy. "Did you know about this, John?" he asked, as he saw John enter the room.

The last thing John needed was to be the center of attention during a Randy-sized flare-up. Not here. Not today. The signs of conflict were everywhere. Blake leaned back in his chair—as though he could dissolve right through the wall. Michelle Zapato, the VP of Sales, was turning bright pink. One man John didn't recognize pulled his collar away from his neck with his left hand and fanned himself with his right. There were throats being cleared, breaths being swallowed. John thought of the chess-board. Randy had made a move, and it clearly affected the other players' next moves.

"Well?" Randy was still waiting for a reply.

"Can this wait for after—"

"No, it can't wait," interrupted Randy. "We're getting thrown under the bus!"

"I don't even know what you're talking about," pleaded John. "Let's table this for a more appropriate—"

"Don't you bail out on me, man," Randy shot back. "This is exactly the appropriate place. We're here to talk about sales. And Leslie's doing her best to stomp on our numbers."

John was trapped in the middle of two firmly entrenched forces and he had no idea what the battle was even about—didn't want to know. He physically and subconsciously took a few steps back. John knew he was withdrawing into Green conflict, and it was only serving to stoke the fire within Randy. John needed to throw himself a rope and pull out of it.

"OK, Randy. This is clearly important for you to discuss. But you gotta clue me in. I just walked in the door."

Randy's shoulders settled slightly. "The Centauri launch. She's canning the campaign."

The news hit John in the gut. "What?"

"I know, right?" said Randy. "There's absolutely no good reason to cancel that campaign. I've got pre-orders on seven customers' desks, just waiting for the official launch."

John noticed a few other sales managers nod in support of Randy. John, himself, had a few pre-orders awaiting the launch. He felt a flash of envy on hearing of Randy's seven. Impressive. John had promised pre-orders with at least two customers—maybe three. Cancellation of the campaign would mean a lot of creative and unpleasant storytelling. Or worse, customer complaints about unfulfilled orders for a product they weren't even supposed to know about. John looked over at Leslie, who seemed to be waiting for John's reaction with bated breath.

"That's... not good," said John, once again fighting the urge to disappear.

"Great. So you're gonna jump on the bandwagon and blame me for blocking your pipeline too?" said Leslie. "Why are you two even talking about Centauri with customers?"

Not only was John deep into conflict, he was fast approaching his second-stage Red.

"You knew damn well that Centauri was getting binned," Leslie asserted.

John's mind was racing. Could Leslie be right? Was this more than just a marketing delay? Was Centauri was being cancelled completely? He needed to call his customers. He needed to locate some kind of e-mail or memo that could be interpreted as permission to pre-sell the product...

"You two actually took orders for it?" asked Gail, joining the fray.

John was suddenly very aware that he and Randy were the only ones standing in a room of fifty people. Second-stage Red in this setting could wind up being corporate suicide. With a deep breath, John collected himself. While actual orders before the launch were clearly against the rulebook, there was a longstanding and widespread practice of letting top clients "pre-order." He calmly looked over at Randy—his nose flaring, the imaginary Red glow beating with intensity.

"Randy, I don't think you were the only one in here caught off-guard. We saw a great opportunity, and we went after it. It's what makes you great at what you do."

John glanced at Michelle, the VP, and continued, "Ultimately, we need to do what's right for the customer and deal with whatever the decision is regarding Centauri."

"I want to know now," Randy demanded.

"It's not the time, Randy. I believe this meeting already has an agenda," said John, "and we should respect that. And respect the many people in this room—many of whom traveled a good distance to be here." He looked Randy in the eyes, "Can we address this after?"

Randy was already sitting down. "Sure. As long as we do it soon."

John turned to Gail. "I think there may be a lack of clarity in our new product procedures. Perhaps you can be a part of that discussion, Gail?"

"I would be glad to," replied Gail, uncrossing her arms.

John looked at Leslie. "You good with that? Group up after the meeting today?"

"That works," she said.

John's eyes found Michelle again. Her face was returning to a more normal color, and her fidgeting had subsided. He guessed she had found herself in Blue conflict, though she hadn't said a word. John thought about how to create a comfortable hand off as he found the last open chair and took a seat.

"My apologies, Michelle. I know this probably wasn't the opener you had in mind. We sometimes like to improv a little."

She and a few others in the room chuckled. It was more of a pressure release than a genuine laugh, but it seemed to serve its purpose.

"No problem," said Michelle, standing.

"Yeah, things have just been a little tense around here lately," said Randy, with a glint of embarrassment flashing in his eyes.

John wondered if Randy meant that as an apology.

"Well then," said Michelle, "let's share a little good news, shall we?" Her voice was bright and cheery, as she attempted to sweep away the tension from the room.

John smiled, awash with pride. It had been a brutal, public display of conflict, and he had somehow managed to wrestle control of his own feelings. He had also been able to guide Randy and everyone else involved back to a more productive place. He glanced over at Gail, who offered an approving nod.

It was an exciting win for him. His mind wandered as Michelle droned on about revenue and projections. The graph on the slide clearly showed Starr's sales success—just slightly ahead of target.

Out of the corner of his eye, John saw someone enter the room. But it was the pause in Michelle's speech that most piqued his curiosity. John tried to make out the dark figure standing at the back of the room, but the light from the projector obscured his view.

"Welcome," said Michelle. "I'm glad you could join us, Mr. Keyes."

Everyone seemed to turn at once. There he was. The infamous Philip Keyes. John leaned over, trying to actually see the man's face.

"Proceed," said Keyes. "I'm only here to observe."

John's mind raced again: Did the VP know that Keyes was coming? If Keyes was expected, why wasn't it on the agenda? Was this an intentional ambush? What was going on?

Michelle continued her uplifting presentation with a degree of awkwardness and formality that wasn't there before. Even the VPs are scared of this guy, John thought to himself. She went on and on about exceeding sales targets and cited several examples of Starr's best clients. She was in the middle of a gushing review of Starr's performance in the Midwest, when Keyes finally interrupted.

"OK, got it. But what problems are you experiencing?"

The question was met with total silence. He stepped forward and repeated the question. "What problems are you experiencing?"

Michelle looked at the screen, as if the answer might be hidden there. Keyes surveyed the room full of executives. They avoided his eye like a group of unprepared students praying not to be called on.

The only problem John was experiencing was how to turn invisible in this meeting.

"Incredible," said Keyes, sharply. He placed his fists knuckles-down on the table and leaned in. "You may be 5-percent above your top-line revenue goal—Bravo! But you people aren't even halfway to profit expectations. You know what that is? Unsustainable."

Keyes started pacing again. "What's going on in this department? Employee turnover is trending up... We're losing good people around here almost every day. And *nobody* has any problems?"

Silence.

"Well, I have a problem!" continued Keyes. "I have a problem with contracts that lose money—adding only to revenue targets that create income for salespeople but result in impossible demands for other support people at Starr." He was pacing now. Keyes reminded John of a lawyer addressing a jury with a well-rehearsed closing argument. "I have a problem with contracts like this..."

He reached into the breast pocket of his tailored black jacket and produced some folded papers. The crowd watched with fearful anticipation, as Keyes slowly unfolded them.

"I have a problem with people who sign contracts like this one with EagleMark Enterprises. It's resource-wasting contracts like this that make me wonder what's really going on around here."

He turned to the last page of the contract and read the signature. "My problem is with Gail R. Townsend."

The conflict in the room was palpable. Keyes followed everyone's eyes to the target of his rage. Gail's own eyes were wide open and full of fear.

"And you must be her," said Keyes, coldly.

Gail remained quiet as Keyes proceeded to recite the flaws of the EagleMark deal. His voice echoed in the background, as John felt himself fall quickly back into conflict. John knew he was the main reason for the Eaglemark fiasco. He had started it and persuaded others that it was a good idea. It really did seem like a good idea at the time. John had recognized the potential right away. And it was still there, just waiting to pop. Gail had initially resisted the whole deal but finally signed it—succumbing to John's relentless badgering and overt confidence. Now, here she was, being publicly berated for it.

If there was going to be a fall-guy, it should be John.

He knew he needed to step up. His conflict "smoke alarm" was screeching in his head and stage two Red was not far behind. He wished an actual fire alarm would go off; he would give anything for just five minutes to think. It was time for action. But what action? Keyes was clearly showing signs of Red conflict. But where was his motivational value system? John yanked himself back to the situation and listened for Keyes' word choice—looking for clues to his location on the triangle.

Keyes held an impressive command of the details surrounding the EagleMark situation: The support staff being taken advantage of, the charges for customized packaging, the unforeseen waste, the administrative staff's resentment of the salespeople for getting paid on revenue targets—while they were left dealing with onerous compliance and unfamiliar government reporting requirements.

John hurriedly began collecting in his head the reasons he was hearing. *Unsustainable... Employee turnover... People being taken advantage of... Waste and poor planning... Burden on staff... Resentment from staff...* John sat up as it hit him. These were Blue and Green reasons—Cautious-Supporting reasons.

Heads turned his way as John stood up from his chair.

"Sir, I convinced Gail to sign that contract."

Keyes slowly turned his attention on him, his eyes burning with disdain.

"And you are...?"

"John Doyle, sir."

John's heart pounded like a bass drum. Keyes' threatening stare melted John's confidence. He felt his knees wobble, and he was about to return to his chair when he began to visualize the glow—bright Blue and Green lights emanating from behind Keyes' head like the spotlights on Mac's stage. The imagery strengthened John's resolve.

"You're correct about that contract in every way," said John. "I'm not proud of it."

"Nor should you be," said Keyes, as he tossed the contract onto the table and walked away. John began to panic.

"I'm still confident that I can make that account profitable, Mr. Keyes," said John with manufactured certainty.

Keyes scoffed at the comment but didn't turn back. *Too Red, Doyle!* John scolded himself. Blue-Green, Blue-Green, Blue-Green...

"And frankly, sir," continued John, "it was an important learning experience for us—for me. I've been taking steps... going through a process to improve the way Gail and I communicate and make decisions."

Keyes stopped and turned. John plowed ahead.

"It's helping us to more fully consider each opportunity and any related risks, so we don't make promises to customers that we can't keep—or that would be cost-prohibitive to keep." John motioned to Gail, "It's also helping the relationship between us."

Keyes let the silence simmer as he considered what he was hearing.

John felt compelled to fill the void. "I'm not proud of what happened on the EagleMark deal so far, but I'm proud of the work we've done together to make sure we don't repeat it."

Keyes looked at Gail. She offered a confirming nod.

"Doyle, Townsend, walk with me," commanded Keyes, as he pushed through the door into the hall. Gail and John shared a terrified look as the meeting room door closed behind him with a sharp, metallic clank.

* * *

They found Keyes waiting for an elevator in the lobby. John didn't know what to expect. His limbs felt numb, and his head was swimming. Was he about to lose his job? As he often did, John felt compelled to fill the silence—this time with a Blue-Green translation of his earlier Red outburst...

"Mr, Keyes, it's my personal mission to salvage that contract and bring in the revenue to justify the sacrifices that the people in this company have made to—"

"OK, Doyle," said Keyes with the hint of a smile. "Stand down." The intensity was gone from his voice.

"Sorry," said John, a little embarrassed.

"You took a stand in there, Doyle. I can respect that."

"Thank you, sir."

"Are you really committed to honoring the sacrifices that the good people at this company are making?"

"Absolutely."

"And I assume you have a plan for this?"

"We do, yes," said John.

Keyes studied him closely.

"I hope so. I'll be watching this account—and you—with interest. Mistakes are going to happen, John. Believe me. I've made some eight-figure mistakes myself. The key is always to grow from it—learn from it."

"Absolutely, sir," said Gail.

They were both surprised to hear Gail's voice. *Welcome back*, thought John to himself.

Keyes shook John's hand and looked him squarely in the eye. "A hero of mine once said, 'The ultimate measure of a man is not where he stands in moments of comfort and convenience, but where he stands at times of challenge and controversy.'"

"Who said that, sir?" asked John.

The elevator chimed, and Keyes stepped inside.

"Martin Luther King, Jr."

* * *

Gail closed the door to John's office, as John put his phone on 'do not disturb' mode. He started to pace; sitting didn't feel like an option. He was still feeling numb—maybe a little too excited to sit just yet.

"Should we get back to the meeting?" asked Gail.

"Eh, let 'em wonder a little longer," said John with a big smile.

"John, I'm *really* impressed," said Gail, sincerely, "and grateful. I'm not sure what I just witnessed there—hypnosis or mind-reading."

"Listening, mostly," said John.

"No, that was me. I just sat and stared like a fool."

"You fell into conflict is all. I did, too, but I yanked myself back out. He's a pretty intimidating guy."

Gail settled into one of John's guest chairs. "You can say that again."

"All I did was appeal to what seemed to be important to him."

"How?"

"What I heard—beneath all that anger—was a man who was all about fairness and people."

"I could see that, I guess. Toward the end," said Gail. "But when did you figure it out?"

"Well, it helps to know what to listen for," said John. "When he was talking about those problems in the meeting, he was in conflict—aggressive and challenging. But the reasons he was in conflict had to do with people being taken advantage of or wastefulness and poor planning. So I guessed that his assertive conflict response had been triggered by violations of cautious and supporting values."

"Huh. But how did you know what to say?"

"Once I figured out what mattered to him, I just found a way of telling the truth in a way that was respectful of his values."

Gail nodded slowly, absorbing every word carefully.

"It's about finding out what's important to people, respecting it, and then using the right skills to address the person's needs—even before you present what's important to you. If you can do that, you're better positioned to find good solutions that resolve the conflict and help both parties to feel good about themselves."

"All I can say is," said Gail, "if you can master the approach you've just described, I think you'll have no problem going places in this company. And if EagleMark actually comes through for us—even better."

"I think a lot of things are going to be better," said John.

He had finally calmed down enough to sit. It was hard to believe it had only been a few weeks since he sat in this same chair, feeling the walls crashing down around him. The events of the day he was denied promotion had shaken him to the core. The confidence that was so important to his self-worth had been stripped bare, and he found himself questioning his very identity.

As John sat, sharing a friendly, victorious moment with his one-time foe, Gail, he recognized that the worst day of his career had really been the best. It had been the punch he needed to knock him out of his unproductive ways and into action that was sure to take him to a much better place. His goals suddenly seemed attainable again. In fact, maybe those outdated goals were too attainable. But even more fulfilling, John found an unexpected strength and excitement in his new attitude toward his relationships. People were no longer obstacles in the way of his goals—they were partners that made the journey more rewarding.

STARR
INDUSTRIES

Dr. Mac Wilson
5155 Front Street

Star-It Fax Note   79□1

Date	# of pages ▸ 2
From *John Doyle*	
Co./Dept.	Co.
Phone #	Phone #
Fax #	Fax #

Hi, Theodore ;-)

It may sound odd, but I was thinking about you last week, as Nancy and I celebrated our 15th wedding anniversary in Italy. It was an amazing trip, and our relationship feels stronger than ever. We truly feel we have you to thank for that. My greater sense of awareness has helped me to recognize when I'm moving into conflict, and I'm able to articulate my feelings to Nancy without pulling away. She appreciates my willingness to let her into my world and help me sort through it all.

Thanks again for setting Nancy up with her own assessments. The information has been invaluable to our relationship. We're having some great conversations again—much like when we were dating. Not to say there isn't still conflict in our marriage. Nancy's consulting work has really taken off, and our lives are as busy as ever. Those Red and Blue filters definitely get in the way from time-to-time. But I'm getting much better at not accepting every invitation to conflict, and I'm finally recognizing Nancy's more subtle conflict triggers. When things do get heated between us, I've started asking her why the issue is so important to her. Just hearing her answer allows me to borrow an effective behavior more quickly. You'll be glad to know I'm reaching down into those middle and lower drawers of my toolbox much more frequently, and it's amazing how much more civil and productive our conversations are now. Nancy's using this approach as well. It's like we've learned a new language.

Hard to believe it's almost been a year since our last appointment. So much has happened in my life... The big one you might be curious about is that elusive promotion at Starr Industries. Well, I guess third time's a charm. I'm a regional director! ...which basically means I super-sized my team and my area of responsibility. I'm really enjoying the new role and the people I'm working with. I love the challenges and have developed some solid relationships right away.

My rise to regional director also makes Gail and I peers. I've truly come to appreciate her thoughtful approach and often use her as a sounding board for new ideas. Believe it or not, she even asked me recently to turn one of her notoriously verbose presentations into ten bullet points for her.

I'm also Randy's boss now. It was pretty awkward at first, and some of our jokes got a little too personal. We had one ugly blowout, which really revealed how a conflict between two people can bring down a whole team. But I was able to resolve it with an apology to the team and a heart-to-heart with Randy. We're on excellent terms again and only trade insults after hours. And as far as the team as a whole, we might actually be stronger, now that we've been in the foxhole together and survived.

I hope you're doing well, and for the sake of the world, I hope you're still busy as ever.

Sincerely,

JDoyle

John Doyle
Regional Director of Sales

JOHN'S NOTEBOOK

a summary of learning

Have a Nice Conflict...!?!

1:00pm Thursday
5155 Front Street

The <u>soft stuff</u> is harder than the hard stuff (Soft skills)

Do conflict. Don't let it do you.
Don't be a victim to it!

Everyone is in
the people business.

Conflict has potential...
the potential to be prevented
—OR—
the potential to be beneficial

*Learn to manage conflict & build relationships
for better results

Call Jenny @ Mac's office
555-3800

Strength Deployment Inventory

↓

Portrait of Personal Strengths

*Don't forget
to thank
Walter

Saturday 10:00am
6300 Fairhaven Dr.

Prevent Conflict before it happens!

Conflict is opportunity to step back & assess...
find creative solutions

No one-size-fits-all answer for
dealing with people in conflict

Try to:
+ work well with people
+ help people feel worthwhile
+ meet them where they're at
+ build the relationship whenever you can

"The most important single ingredient in the formula
of success is knowing how to get along with people"

  *Teddy Roosevelt

  *Takes more than being good
  at your job to achieve success

—We don't get an owner's manual for our relationships.
  We've got to figure them out on our own!

—We can look at people's behavior, but it's not the
  whole story!

—The key is identifying "why" people do what they do.
  More worthwhile to understand their reason for using
  behavior. Intent... Motivation!

202

Personal Strengths:

- behaviors that enhance Self-Worth
  (our own & other peoples')
- the different ways a person can interact with others

- make us feel good about ourselves and make
  us feel like we're contributing
- support our underlying motivation or set of values

We always have the ability to choose
our behavior — the right tool for the job!

If I use what's convenient
for me, it may take twice as
long to fix the problem...

—or— I may do damage!

CENTER AREA of Portrait

Lots of behavior options available
that aren't so painful to choose!

— You're most effective when choosing a strength
that enhances the self-worth of others while
helping achieve your own self-worth.

— Try to see the world from another person's
perspective. My way isn't the only way.

Take Control!

— be in charge of your own behavior.

— choose what's right for the situation and
the person you're with

— Behavior has consequences
— Choice creates accountability.

>...but allows us to influence what happens in our relationships — have more control of our lives/careers

good choices —> good outcomes
poor choices —> poor results in —> so we're not getting
　　　　　　　　our relationships　　what we want!

A Personal Strength can cause conflict when it's <u>Overdone</u>

Overdone Strengths:
— strengths we favor can become weaknesses when overdone or misused

— a behavior that denies self-worth to self or others

— includes actually overdone or perceived as overdone.

MY STRENGTHS　...if OVERDONE Becomes:

My Strengths	Becomes
Self-confident —>	Arrogant
Competitive —>	Combative
Ambitious —>	Ruthless
Fair —>	Unfeeling
Quick to Act —>	Rash
Principled —>	Unbending

Just need "volume" control!

—Conflict can happen when other people misinterpret your strengths

— People are almost always trying to do good and seeking feelings of self-worth

Annoying Behavior in others?

- look for the strength behind it
- What are they overdoing?
- What are they really trying to accomplish?
- Try to understand them better
- Understanding helps avoid misperceptions

All it takes is
  Insight...
   Practice...
   and the realization
   that you have a Choice!

GETTING FEEDBACK

List your top six strengths and their definitions using the Portrait of Personal Strengths you completed. Ask at least three people who are important to you *(i.e., spouse or significant other, boss, direct report, or key coworkers or customers)* if they might be willing to give you some honest feedback. Explain that you are working to become more effective in your work and personal relationships and better at managing conflict. The conversation can be as brief as only 5 minutes. Further explain that you sincerely want their candor and you promise not to hold anything they say against them. Make sure that the conversation is private and you might consider having it over coffee (your treat).

If they agree, share at least three of your top six strengths with them and ask them to provide an example of how you used each of the strengths to positively affect your relationship or your work together. Ask them to be as specific as possible so you can connect their feedback to specific behaviors.

Next, remind your feedback providers to be honest and ask them if there are also examples of when your application of these strengths might have hurt your relationship, led to conflict, or did not benefit a project. Ask them to be as specific as possible. You might also ask them how it made them feel at the time.

— Do not be defensive or offer explanations
— Just smile and say thank you!

What's my motivation?
What's their motivation?

> — Where are other people coming from?

> — What are they after?

> — For productive relationships, we need to know what our motivation is and what the <u>other person's</u> motivation is

Most important to know "why" someone is doing something...
- to understand their intent
- avoid letting misinterpretations cause you conflict
- respect where they're coming from

<u>Filters:</u>

We interpret what we see others do through our own set of standards...

AND we assume everyone views the world the way we do! Most often, they don't... Cause of conflict!

Misinterpretation

Motivational Value Systems: ⟶

- differing clusters of motives when things are going well
- serving our desire to feel good about ourselves (self-worth)
- blends of values that work together to drive our behavior

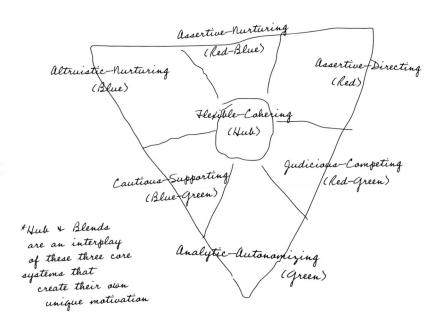

Assertive-Nurturing
(Red-Blue)

Altruistic-Nurturing
(Blue)

Assertive-Directing
(Red)

Flexible-Cohering
(Hub)

Judicious-Competing
(Red-Green)

Cautious-Supporting
(Blue-Green)

*Hub & Blends
are an interplay
of these three core
systems that
create their own
unique motivation

Analytic-Autonomizing
(Green)

— within each of these seven, there's variation
— the colors mix in varying degrees
— even two people in the Red area may have
varying degrees of Red

This diversity is good

*While we're trying to do the "right thing" to
maintain our self-worth, conflict can happen when
our "right thing" appears to be the "wrong thing" to
another person across the triangle

— our motivations are filtering our perceptions
— we feel conflict when we see behaviors that
challenge our way of doing things
— our styles are so different we feel like we're
working against each other

*Conflict can be prevented by seeing contentious behavior as merely a difference of style instead of a direct challenge or threat aimed at annoying you or derailing you.

Conflict is a choice
just like behavior is a choice...
  - you know they're just trying to do what they feel is right
  - they're using behaviors that bring them self-worth
  - if you still let it get to you, that's your choice

Conflict is different from Opposition
When people have disagreements about how to handle an issue, that's "opposition"

  - Opposition is often part of a healthy debate that leads to better ideas
  - Conflict occurs when a person feels their sense of self-worth is at risk...   it gets personal!

> Conflict is that feeling that occurs when another person or set of circumstances becomes an obstacle that inhibits your ability to live out your motivational values

What happens in Conflict? (self-worth being threatened)
  - your motivation can change completely
  - you experience sequential changes in your motivation which drive changes in your behavior
  - you enter your Conflict Sequence ⟶

209

Conflict Sequence:

predictable pattern... a sequence of 3 progressively serious stages often evident to others due to a change in your behavior

Stage 1: your attention is focused on yourself, the Problem, and the Other Person

Stage 2: the focus narrows to yourself and the Problem
(the other person has dropped out of the picture)

Stage 3: the focus is only on Self.
— This is the most damaging stage because the individual has lost sight of the Problem and the Other Person
— Many only experience Stage 3 a handful of times... not pleasant!

13 different Conflict Sequences (combinations of Blue, Red, and green)

Blue = being accomodating
Red = rising to the challenge
Green = being cautious & analytical

2 people in conflict might have different conflict sequences and they don't necessarily cycle through their sequences at the same time.

*Because people only go into conflict about things that are important to them, it's a great opportunity to learn what's important to them
...and therefore learn how to communicate better in the future

Conflict can't be eliminated completely BUT...
— we can prevent conflicts that are preventable
— manage conflicts that are inevitable
— minimize visits to your deeper stages of conflict
— conflict can actually enhance your relationships

But keep it in Stage One!
In Stage 2 or 3, you've no longer concerned about the relationship.

210

Tuesday 2:00 p.m.
Memorial Pier, Rockway Beach

Conflict doesn't have to be between people—all it
takes is your self-worth being threatened

Note to self:
I suck at fishing

*For BEST Results:
Respect people's motivational value system
and deliver your message in their language

5 Keys to having a nice conflict
1) Anticipate
2) Prevent
3) Identify
4) Manage
5) Resolve

Be on the lookout
for it. Expect it!

Anticipate Conflict:
Ask yourself how people with different motivational
values might view a situation. When two or more people
see things differently, there's conflict potential.

Consider People's Conflict Triggers...

— words or actions that might threaten their
self-worth and push them into conflict

— know their motivational values, you can
guess what might trigger conflict in them and
be better prepared to respond

How to figure out
someone's Motivational
Value System:
(what "language" they're speaking)

— inquiry and observation
— discover the "why." Why is that
important to you? Why do you like
working here? Why does that bug you?
— their answers will reveal their values
— REMEMBER: takes more than
one data point to show a trend

211

Prevent Conflict:

- A well-chosen behavior on your part can prevent conflict with another person
- Figure out how to get your intent across in a way that the other person can relate to and won't be misinterpreted
- Take steps to prevent your behaviors from coming across as overdone
- Refine your communication by using your top strengths appropriately or by "Borrowing"

> **Borrowing:**
> Using a non-preferred behavior that is less likely to trigger conflict and more likely to lead to productive results in a relationship.

*Preventing conflict is about the deliberate, appropriate use of strengths in your relationships. It's about knowing the people in my life better and interacting with them in a more productive way.

Also...
Prevent conflict in yourself by being careful of how you choose to perceive other people's behavior.

Identify Conflict:

Look for clues to conflict in yourself and others

Learn to spot the three basic approaches to conflict:

- Blue accommodating
- Red rising to the challenge
- Green cautious analysis.

The Conflict Sequence shows up in different ways for different people.

212

—Spot the shift in motivation/subtle clues of conflict...

—Can be difficult with someone whose conflict color is so
  close to their motivational value system. *like Nancy
  (Blue MVS + 1st
  Stage Blue in Conflict)

—Raise your awareness so you can
  identify it in stage one...

Avoid the pain and suffering of stage 2 or 3!

Ask sincere, appropriate questions with
  the intent of preventing or managing
  conflict — Never a bad idea...

Friday 8:00a.m.
Starling Cafe

Manage Conflict:

- Approach people based on how they are feeling in the conflict. (Blue, Red, or Green)
- Find out what's important to them, respect that—and then introduce what's important to you.
- Manage Yourself and Manage the Relationship
- Create the conditions where the other person can manage themselves.

* It's hard to dislike a person that you know. When you take the time to get to know a person at a level where you understand their motives, values and their sources of self-worth and esteem, you are less likely to find yourself in conflict.

Conflict is an emotional state between people.

Resolve Conflict:

to create movement toward resolution we need to show them the path back to self-worth.

Have a Nice Conflict

To keep a relationship going, you've got to manage the conflict so that the threats to self-worth are removed and resolve it so the results of the conflict confirm each person's self-worth.

The 5 keys to conflict put you in a better position to:

- find good solutions
- resolve the conflict
- help both parties to feel good about themselves
- enhance and build relationships

"The ultimate measure of a man
is not where he stands in moments of
comfort and convenience, but where
he stands at times of
challenge and controversy."

Martin Luther King Jr.

Have a Nice Conflict

T.R. MAC WILSON, Ph.D.

AUTHOR'S NOTE: In conceiving this story, we wanted to be consistent with our own beliefs about personal and organizational development. Toward that end, we have crafted a statement of philosophy, written from the perspective of our character, Dr. Mac.

Philosophy of Personal and Organizational Developme

It is important to me that I work w
organizations and individuals who
share, or at a minimum, respect, n
philosophy of personal and organi:
I have written this paper to expres:
provide references to significant thinkers who have helped
to shape it, and to increase the probability of structuring
relationships with clients where I can facilitate
meaningful change.

Organizational Systems and Leadership

I believe that organizations are social systems. Therefore,
the quality of working life cannot be improved without also
considering the human element. A deep understanding of
oneself is a prerequisite to understanding relationships,
which are the fabric of the organization's social system.

To be sustainable, organizations (whether public, private,
government, or for-profit) must know how they contribute
to making the world (or their part of it) a better place while
accomplishing their stated goals. "In tumultuous times,
we urgently need leaders who will mobilize people for the
common good. Leadership always implies a relationship
between leader and led, and that relationship exists within

a *context*. To understand leadership in context, we have to place ourselves within that culture and get inside the heads of the people a would-be leader is trying to mobilize." (Maccoby, 2007)

Conflict Management

"It is impossible to understand people, their emotional and mental states, without understanding the nature of value and moral conflicts." (Fromm, 1947) Conflict can be a source of great productivity and restored relationships or the source of destructive stress and waste of resources. The word conflict is used, in the English language, to describe too wide a range of issues, from simple disagreements to bitter and destructive patterns in relationships and war between countries. Therefore, I use as a definition of *conflict*: When a person is faced with a situation that threatens their sense of self-worth or value. (Porter, 1996) I use the word *opposition* to describe situations where people disagree or have opposing views that do not involve a threat to a person's sense of self-worth. Managing conflict requires, primarily, an understanding of people, whereas managing opposition requires, primarily, an understanding of the issues. The goal of conflict management is to remove the value-based threats to self-worth, so opposition can be managed by people in their most productive state of being.

Conditions Conducive to Change

I am typically invited to work with people in an organization because they perceive a need for a change and have a desire for better results within the organization; however results are defined for that organization. I am not an expert in strategy, process improvement, or other essential business areas. My expertise lies in creating relationships that are conducive to productive change. Whether taking on the role of a coach to an individual, a facilitator for a group experience, or an ongoing consultative relationship that moves the culture of the entire organization, I see my job as creating the environment where change can happen. My philosophy in this regard has been heavily influenced by Carl Rogers (1961) and I present my own slight adaptation of his ideas here:

If I can create a relationship characterized on my part by:

- genuineness and transparency, in which I am congruent in my experience, awareness, and communication

- acceptance and unconditional regard for each individual with whom I work or each person within a team or organization

- my ability to see each person or team as they see themselves

then other people (individuals or teams) will respond to this relationship by becoming:

- more fully aware of themselves
- better integrated and more able to function effectively
- more like the individual, team, or organization they would like to be
- more self-directing and less reliant on extrinsic motivation
- more able to understand and accept others
- more able to manage conflict productively.

Accountability

I believe that long-term accountability cannot be imposed or demanded; it occurs as an inevitable outgrowth of personal freedom. "We account for what we choose and what we claim as our own. As an inevitable consequence of our freedom, we are forced to experience and confront our anxiety over the choices we make." (Koestenbaum, 2001) Ironically, and difficult for many people to accept, the more we provide choice, within certain logical boundaries, the more we actually end up creating accountability, and the more we gain other's permission to use control when the situation calls for it. To effectively frame choice in the context of an organization, we must have a clear purpose and definition of results, clear positive and negative consequences, and the ability to administer both positive and negative consequences. Part of the role of a leader is to confront followers with their freedom, thereby engaging them in choice and increasing accountability. Choice also taps into intrinsic motivation, which is a much more powerful and sustainable drive than extrinsic motivation. (Deci, 1995)

Personality Models

I use the Strength Deployment Inventory (SDI) to facilitate self-discovery and generate pictures of relationships. I use the SDI almost exclusively because it:

- is based on a theory of relationships

- views personality as a system of motivations

- makes it easier for people to makes choices in their relationships that are intended to get productive results

- honors the self-worth of people and explains the source of conflict as threats to self-worth
- accounts for changes in motivation in the face of continuing conflict
- does not typecast or stereotype people
- links with feedback and expectations versions that allow me to create pictures of how people perceive each other and what they expect from each other in the context of specific working relationships
- is simple, memorable, and easy to understand on the surface, yet also provides the deepest self-discovery experience.

Attitudes Are More Important Than Techniques

Behavior is a surface-level issue. Behavior arises from core beliefs, motivations, assumptions, perceptions, intentions, etc. To change behavior, we need to work below the surface. A lot of behavior-change attempts fail because they try to change only the behavior, without thinking about what drives that behavior. Techniques are still important, but they will not be self-sustaining unless they are connected to beliefs.

Humor and Fun

Some of the worst work experiences involve destructive, conflict-ridden relationships. Injecting some fun and humor into serious situations can serve as a safety-valve, releasing some of the pressure. Work should be fun, and some of the most enjoyable parts of work are in the context of productive relationships.

To become fully ourselves, we must enjoy our work and we must enjoy the process of learning. We all have an innate drive to play, and when our work cuts off or restricts our play drive, we may find ourselves unable to learn (Maccoby, 1995) or in conflict with the environment or the person we perceive to have created that environment. To paraphrase Sigmund Freud (Brill, 1995): Humor can help people to feel better about themselves by satisfying needs that cannot be met in certain situations, and opening a window to learning about these situations.

References

Brill, A. (1995). *The basic writings of Sigmund Freud: Wit and its relations to the unconscious.* New York: Random House, Modern Library Edition.

Deci, E. (1995). *Why we do what we do: Understanding self-motivation.* New York: Penguin Books.

Fromm, E. (1947). *Man for himself: An inquiry into the psychology of ethics.* New York: Henry Holt and Company.

Koestenbaum, P., Block, P. (2001). *Freedom and accountability at work: Applying philosophic insight to the real world.* San Francisco: Jossey-Bass/Pfeiffer.

Maccoby, M (1995). *Why work? Motivating the new workforce* (2nd ed.). Alexandria, Virginia: Miles River Press.

Maccoby, M. (2007). *The leaders we need and what makes us follow.* Boston: Harvard Business School Publishing.

Porter, E. (1996). *Relationship Awareness Theory: Manual of administration and interpretation* (9th ed.). Carlsbad, California: Personal Strengths Publishing.

Rogers, C. (1961). *On becoming a person.* New York: Houghton Mifflin.

CHARACTER
ASSESSMENT
RESULTS

THE PERSONALITIES of the fictional characters presented in this book are consistent with the personality descriptions presented in the SDI® (Strength Deployment Inventory®). There are seven Motivational Value Systems, derived from various combinations of three primary drives in relationships. Your Motivational Value System acts as an internal filter through which life is interpreted and understood. It is a unifying set of values for choosing behavior that enhances your sense of self-worth. What follows are more detailed descriptions of each Motivational Value System as described in Dr. Elias H. Porter's theory of Relationship Awareness.®

THE 7 MOTIVATIONAL VALUE SYSTEMS

BLUE: Altruistic–Nurturing
- Concern for the protection, growth, and welfare of others

RED: Assertive–Directing
- Concern for task accomplishment
- Concern for organization of people, time, money, and any other resources to achieve desired results

GREEN: Analytic–Autonomizing
- Concern for assurance that things have been properly thought out
- Concern for meaningful order being established and maintained

HUB: Flexible–Cohering
- Concern for flexibility
- Concern for members of the group, the welfare of the group, and belonging in the group

RED-BLUE: Assertive–Nurturing
- Concern for the protection, growth, and welfare of others through task accomplishment and leadership

RED-GREEN: Judicious–Competing
- Concern for intelligent assertiveness, justice, leadership, order, and fairness in competition

BLUE-GREEN: Cautious–Supporting
- Concern for affirming and developing self-sufficiency in self and others
- Concern for thoughtful helpfulness with regard for justice

MAIN CHARACTERS

The fictional SDI results of our four main characters (presented below) served as a guide for describing their motives, behaviors and perceptions when things were going well, and during conflict.

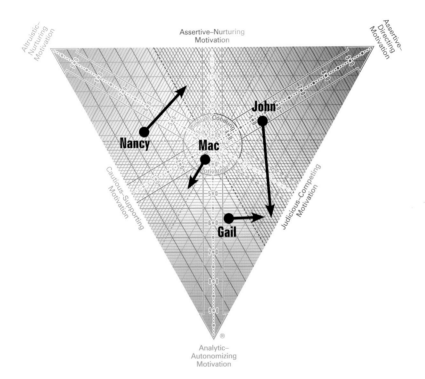

Individuals who complete an SDI receive their results in the form of arrows on the interaction triangle. The dots represent the Motivational Value Systems, while the arrowheads represent the Conflict Sequences.

CONFLICT SEQUENCE

The Conflict Sequence describes internal changes in feelings and motives in response to perceived threats. While people most frequently use behavior that looks very similar to they way they are feeling, other behavior choices are always available.

Internal Experience in Conflict

Conflict Stage	Focus is on:	BLUE	RED	GREEN
Stage 1	Self Problem Other	Simply being accommodating to the needs of others	Simply rising to the challenge being offered	Simply being prudently cautious
Stage 2	Self Problem ~~Other~~	Giving in and letting the opposition have its way	Having to fight off the opposition	Trying to escape from the opposition
Stage 3	Self ~~Problem~~ ~~Other~~	Having been completely defeated	Having to fight for one's life	Having to retreat completely

Observable Behavior in Conflict

Conflict Stage	BLUE	RED	GREEN
Stage 1	Accommodate others	Rise to the challenge	Be prudently cautious
Stage 2	Surrender conditionally	Fight to win	Pull back and analyze
Stage 3	Surrender completely	Fight for survival	Withdraw

SUMMARY OF CHARACTER SDI RESULTS

John	Mac	Gail	Nancy
Motivational Value Systems results			
RED Assertive– Directing	**HUB** Flexible– Cohering	**GREEN** Analytic– Autonomizing	**BLUE** Altruistic– Nurturing
Conflict Sequence results			
G-R-B	**G-B-R**	**G-R-B**	**B-R-G**
Wanting to be prudently cautious	Wanting to be prudently cautious	Wanting to be prudently cautious	Wanting to accommodate the needs of others
Wanting to prevail against the issue and/or person	Wanting to partially defer to the other person	Wanting to prevail against the issue and/or person	Wanting to prevail against the issue and/or person
Feeling a need to give up completely	Feeling a need to fight for one's life	Feeling a need to give up completely	Feeling a need to retreat completely

SUPPORTING CHARACTERS

Below are the fictional SDI results for some of our supporting characters. The triangle is a useful tool for quickly identifying where people are coming from and anticipating what might trigger conflict between people.

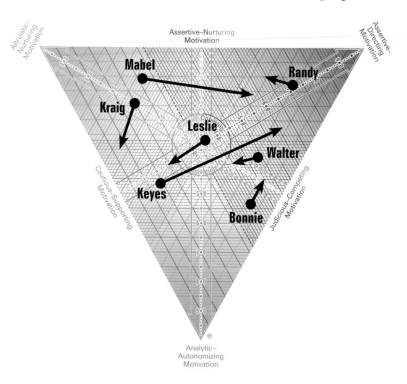

The Strength Deployment Inventory was developed to help people access, understand, and make practical use of Relationship Awareness Theory. When you complete the SDI, you learn about your values that underlie your behaviors in two types of conditions: when all is going well, and when things are in conflict. With this knowledge, you will better understand yourself and the people in your life.

WHERE'S YOUR ARROW?

Now that you've had a taste of Relationship Awareness Theory, you are invited to complete an SDI of your own and experience a personalized debrief call with an expert. Go to the following web link:

http://www.HaveaNiceConflict.com/SDIoffer
enter coupon code 380011 to receive a discount

CONTINUING
THE JOURNEY

WOULD HAVING A NICE CONFLICT benefit your organization or team? Visit www.HaveaNiceConflict.com to learn about the *Have a Nice Conflict* learning experience from Personal Strengths Publishing, Inc.

Also available from Personal Strengths are programs in leadership, mediation, and project management. SDI and other Relationship Awareness assessments integrate in nearly any kind of training initiative. Call to learn how to apply and customize these concepts for your specific needs and goals.

Personal Strengths Publishing, Inc.
P.O. Box 2605, Carlsbad, CA 92018 USA
www.PersonalStrengths.com
+1.760.602.0086

Personal Strengths Publishing, Inc. is based in Carlsbad, California, USA and serves customers through a global network of interrelated distributors who offer products and services consistent with the ideas in this book. The capabilities of these distributors are in three main categories:

1. **Training & Development Services:** direct training for teams and individuals.

2. **Train the Trainer Services:** SDI Certification, co-facilitation, and curriculum design.

3. **SDI & related products:** self-assessments, workplace learning tools, books, video, and other paper and electronic resources. The SDI is available in over 20 languages.

SDI assessments are available for use by certified facilitators who successfully complete the SDI Certification training. Facilitators may be independent or employed by any type of organization. As such, training and development services that incorporate the SDI are available from many individual consultants and large consulting organizations. The capacity for delivery of these services can also be developed within an organization's training, human resources, organization development, or other similar departments.

For more information, find your regional distributor from our web site: **www.PersonalStrengths.com**

FOR MORE INFORMATION

Have a Nice Conflict learning experience:

www.HaveaNiceConflict.com

SDI and other Relationship Awareness assessments:

Personal Strengths Publishing, Inc.
P.O. Box 2605, Carlsbad, CA 92018 USA
www.PersonalStrengths.com
+1.760.602.0086

PERSONAL
STRENGTHS
PUBLISHING